Life's Odd Moments

Life's Odd Moments

Stuart Trueman

with story illustrations by the author

McClelland and Stewart

The Canadian Publishers
McClelland and Stewart Limited
25 Hollinger Road, Toronto M4B 3G2

Canadian Cataloguing in Publication Data

Trueman, Stuart, 1911 –
   Life's odd moments

ISBN 0-7710-8599-0

1. Canadian wit and humor (English)   * I. Title.

PS8539.R83L54 1984   C817 '.54   C84-099170-3
PR9199.3.T78L54 1984

Printed and bound in Canada by John Deyell Company

Acknowledgements

Many of the light-hearted stories in this book are new; some are adapted from Stuart Trueman's popular columns in *The Telegraph-Journal*, Saint John, New Brunswick; others first appeared in *Weekend*, the *Saturday Evening Post*, and other Canadian and United States magazines.

Books by Stuart Trueman

Cousin Elva, 1955;
reissued in 1977 in paperback

The Ordeal of John Gyles, 1966;
reissued in 1973 in paperback;
again reissued in 1984 (New Brunswick Bicentennial Edition)

You're Only As Old As You Act, 1969;
Stephen Leacock Award for Humour

An Intimate History of New Brunswick, 1970;
reissued in 1972 in paperback

My Life As a Rose-Breasted Grosbeak, 1972

The Fascinating World of New Brunswick, 1973;
reissued in 1980 in paperback

Ghosts, Pirates and Treasure Trove, 1975;
reissued in 1981 in paperback

The Wild Life I've Led, 1976

Tall Tales and True Tales from Down East, 1979

The Colour of New Brunswick, 1981

Don't Let Them Smell the Lobsters Cooking, 1982;
reissued in 1983 in paperback

Favorite Recipes from Old New Brunswick Kitchens, 1983

Contents

Clinching the Sale

I've had a most interesting talk with Horace Brashby. He is a salesman. He wanted to sell me lawn seed.

"It's great stuff," he said buoyantly. "Just ask your neighbour Pemberton. Hooked him for a big order yesterday."

"Is that so! Didn't he mind being hooked?"

"Landed him easily," Brashby said obliviously. "Really put the squeeze on him, too – unloaded lawn seed on him, tied him up for vegetable seed, and then what do you think?"

"What?"

"Sewed him up for fertilizer."

He seemed proud of what he had done to Pemberton.

"Roped in Higgins afterward," Brashby went on blithely; "pinned down McAfee, put the bite on Brauwitz, bagged Dunkley the same afternoon. Fourth year in a row I've knocked off Dunkley. Nail him every spring."

"He didn't resist at all?"

The salesman looked somewhat puzzled.

"Why, no; jumped him walking down the street – didn't even have to use pressure. Thought I'd take a crack at Hollingworth today, but he's away. So I came over to give *you* a whirl."

"Good! Would you like to wrestle here or out on the lawn?"

"What do you mean, wrestle?"

Without further preliminaries, as I had already given him fair warning and didn't know much about this sort of thing anyway, I seized him around the middle and whirled him about.

But I hadn't figured on his experience. After he had thumped, slammed, throttled, and gouged me in the proper manner for about three minutes, I was convinced. I bought five pounds of lawn seed.

But at least Brashby won't be able to tell tomorrow's customers I was easy to whirl.

It Takes a Man
To Do It Right

A prominent woman artist in Fredericton, New Brunswick, told me how she and her husband took positive action at last to get rid of raccoons.

The important thing is that the lady in this narrative couldn't get any results at all without her husband's inventive help.

That's the history of the world.

The cute furry raccoons had come out from under the garage every night and overturned the metal garbage container at the back door, scattering litter everywhere.

"It's got to stop!" the husband fulminated.

The lady artist related, "I'd heard that dog food with strong pepper mixed in it would be so nauseating the raccoons would never come back.

"So I mixed it on a platter – and they gobbled it up. They loved it!"

"What did you do then?"

"Well, I made 'bombs' out of paper bags filled with water. In the evening, we watched from an open upstairs window. When the raccoons came, we dropped the bombs on them. They just shook their heads as if it was rain, and went on foraging for food."

Then her husband took charge, as resourceful men down through the ages have had to do.

"I hate to hurt an animal," he said, "but there's no alternative."

He strung an electric wire from the garage across the lawn to the metal garbage container, and turned it on.

"It shouldn't be enough to kill a raccoon," he said, "but it'll give one such a jolt they'll never come back."

That evening they watched again from the upstairs window.

Out from under the garage ambled the fat raccoons – and sat in a semicircle staring warily at the wire.

Something was different, something was new, and they weren't taking any chances.

But, you may ask, did the husband's electric wire finally get results?

It certainly did.

Next morning they heard the garbage truck drive in and then, suddenly, a man's anguished yell:

"Jesus!"

Let Aunt Bessie
Be Your Guide

An object of sympathy among car owners is the fellow who has no maiden great-aunt to take along on family touring trips. He has nobody to watch the highway maps and tell him which is the right road. If he tries to operate the car and watch the maps too, he will certainly put the machine in the ditch. Every maiden great-aunt knows that.

Fortunately the Far Horizons Travel Agency has introduced the idea of renting out respectable elderly ladies to meet this need. It is proving to be a popular service. The wonder is nobody thought of it before.

For instance, I planned to drive from Saint John, New Brunswick, to New York. Never having been past Boston in my life, I signed up "Aunt Bessie" from the agency's stable to navigate the final lap. (That is, of course, her maiden name. Actually I believe she is not a maiden lady, as her name is Mrs. Stanislaus Wrock, and she is not an aunt, as nobody would marry her three sisters. But she has studied her sisters closely and knows what maiden great-aunts will do in a car if they have the chance.)

There are people who claim, "Why it's simple to drive from Boston to New York. It's practically a one-way thoroughfare." I wisely decided not to listen to them. It may *seem* perfectly simple to them because they have maiden great-aunts.

So I settled Aunt Bessie in the back seat, and handed

her all the road maps to spread over her knees, and I was happy to see she immediately took as much interest in worrying about where I was going as though she was my very own. Hardly had I got out of Boston – assuming for the sake of the story that anyone *can* get out of Boston – when she suddenly announced without even looking up from her maps, "We're on the wrong road." That's pretty good service for you!

Startled, I replied I was certain this *was* the road; a sign only a mile back had said Route 153-A.

"Yes," replied Aunt Bessie, "but we went straight; don't suppose the sign might have meant turn left? According to this map we may be on the Ojibway Turnpike. It heads for the Arizona Desert."

There were murmurs of anxiety from the family. After all, they pointed out, Aunt Bessie should know; she had been following the maps ever since the trip started while I'd been squandering my time enjoying the scenery.

I remarked irritably that I remembered this particular stretch of Boston-New York road very well from a picture in the travel folder back at the hotel. But the self-doubt in my voice was audible.

"Judging by these maps," Aunt Bessie persisted, "we'll be entering the Lonely Forest National Park any time now – 150 miles of unbroken wilderness without even a gas station, it says here."

More mutterings of uneasiness in the car. In a desperate attempt to distract Aunt Bessie's attention from her lap, I exclaimed over my shoulder, "Oh, just look! Did you ever see such a beautiful lake as this one we're passing? The sailboats are as pretty as a picture on a calendar!"

But Aunt Bessie couldn't be led astray so easily. She was well aware it would be courting disaster to lift her forefingers off the maps to adjust her trifocals and see the lake, because her fingers might be hundreds of miles off course when she put them down again.

Staring at her knees, she observed: "You say 'a lake.' There is no lake marked on 153-A. We must be on 23-C,

16

heading northwest to join the Alaska Highway. Perhaps I just imagine it, but has anyone else noticed the air getting colder?"

Groans filled the car. Everyone noticed the air had been getting distinctly colder for some time, and they all began to sneeze to prove it.

So I gave in with a sigh and turned left at the next intersection in the hope of finding my way back to 153-A, although my better judgement told me the car had never been off 153-A.

Two hours later we struck the Atlantic coast, where Aunt Bessie, loyal to her principles to the end, resisted all urgings to lift her fingers and admire the fishing boats. Another turn left, she ordered. Two more hours of steady driving – and at long last a big metropolis loomed gleaming on the horizon only twenty miles away. To my relieved eyes it looked like an hospitable and familiar friend. And so it should. It was Boston.

Thus with Aunt Bessie along I recaptured all the excitement and adventure that had been missing from motor trips these last two decades of perfected cars and highways, except of course for those lucky devils who have their own maiden great-aunts to carry in the back seat.

Incidentally, do you remember how you always come back from a trip feeling depressed and sorry it's over, and this always spoils your homecoming? Well, that's only another reason you should patronize the Far Horizons Travel Agency. With Aunt Bessie in the party it was a positive joy to get home. In fact, I could hardly believe it was really possible.

Cheerily I unloaded the family, and locked the car in the garage so she couldn't get out and get into the house before the travel agency sent a taxi for her. It was two days before they got around to it, but Aunt Bessie kept fresh as a daisy in the back seat; I just saw she was well banked daily with new road maps. She was quite happy and could be heard repeatedly saying, as she studied the maps, "We should be coming out of the Hudson Tunnel any minute."

17

Some Kids
Are Just Lucky

Isn't it a riot the silly ways kids figure things out? Little Jimmy, for instance, who's seven, explained to me quite earnestly his method of telling his left hand from his right.

"When the teacher says, 'Everybody hold up their left hand,' " he said, "I look down quick at my hands. The left one is the one with the cat scratches. See it?"

Then he pointed to the little girl with him and commented enviously, "But, boy, Sally's luckier, though! She has marks from *dog* bites. Show him" – she extended her left wrist solemnly – "and everybody knows dog bites last longer than cat scratches. I wish the dog bit *me*."

"Oh, but Charles is really the lucky one," Sally interjected eagerly.

"Golly, yes, he sure is!" Jimmy agreed, and then said to me, by way of fuller information, "Charles is the lucky one, all right."

They took for granted I knew Charles; but I didn't know him or the infallible detection system he followed. I presumed he'd been bitten by a horse, at least.

"What kind of bites does he have?" I asked.

"He hasn't any," Jimmy replied. "He busted his arm last month. When the teacher asks for left hands, he starts to lift up both his arms. The one that feels funny is the left one."

"He's luckier than anybody," Sally sighed. "Scratches and bites don't wear well. They're gone in no time."

"But I wish," Jimmy put in with a tinge of resentment, "he'd stop crowing about his old arm. It's not our fault if we never managed to bust ours."

Aren't children childish? Imagine telling left from right in such absurd ways! They grow out of it, of course. Take an adult like me: I can tell which is my left hand in a split second. Without even thinking. It's the one that has the wrist watch.

How I Ate My Cake and Had It too

I dread dropping in on the Bickhams at Christmas. I can't understand why, because they're always so terribly good to me.

This year, when I thoughtlessly rang their bell to say hello, before I knew it I was sitting on the chesterfield confronted by a plate of chocolate apple-sauce cake.

"You *must* try it," Mrs. Bickham insisted. "*Geraldine* baked it!" This made it a serious matter. Geraldine, who is seven, was watching me. If I didn't try it, they'd think I didn't like Geraldine.

I started eating, while the Bickhams grinned expectantly. The sight of someone eating cake seemed to fascinate them.

"He's not dead *yet*," Mr. Bickham chuckled, puffing his pipe, and the family doubled up with repressed mirth. Even the dog was smiling.

I gulped down my cake and managed to gasp: "It's very nice."

"Have another piece!" Mr. Bickham said heartily, and everyone shrieked. One of the older girls, who was choking over something, fled from the room.

"Now honestly," Mrs. Bickham said, wiping her eyes, "Can you guess what Geraldine did wrong with the chocolate apple-sauce cake recipe?"

I stopped swallowing abruptly.

Judging from the taste, she might have left out the chocolate, or the apple sauce, or possibly the cake. But I had to be diplomatic.

"Did she leave out, er, a pinch of salt?"

Mr. Bickham guffawed. "It's not – ha, ha! – what she *left out*; but it won't – ho, ho, ho! – hurt you."

This touched off delirious screams. I remembered uneasily that only last Christmas Geraldine was making pies out of dead leaves and sand.

Desperately I exclaimed: "Is that *rain* I hear outdoors?"

Everyone looked out; I slipped the remaining piece of cake into my coat pocket.

"Gracious!" said Mrs. Bickham, surprised. "He's eaten the whole plate. Get some more, Geraldine!"

"Oh, please," I began. "I'm full – I –"

"Nonsense! You're *hungry*. Why, we'll send you out of here so fed up you won't eat again for a week!"

That's what I was afraid of, but I couldn't say so.

Now the dog was nosing into my pocket, his head pushing convulsively as he tried to get in deeper.

"He *likes* you," Mrs. Bickham beamed. "They say dogs can sense people's character."

I stood up hurriedly, and yanked out my handkerchief to mop my brow. Pieces of cake flew everywhere.

I was undone; I knew it; I waited for the family's wrath.

Mrs. Bickham shrilled delightedly, "*Look* – he's been hiding away cake to take home! Why on earth didn't you *ask*? Here, Geraldine – put some in a box for him!"

21

I followed Geraldine to the kitchen, hoping she would confess, alone, what she put in.

But I couldn't coax her, the cute little tyke. She just kept giggling irrepressibly while she packed the parcel into an empty dog-food box that smelled strongly like her chocolate apple-sauce cake, which goes to show how a pungent aroma gets into everything in a house.

Birth of
a Best Seller

*Scene: Head office of Midget Popular Books Inc.
Enter a suntanned man in a palm-patterned shirt
and cream-yellow slacks.*

Worried-looking executive at desk: "Welcome back
from your fall vacation in Florida, boss! You're
just in time – we badly need the advice of a discrimi-
nating literary mind like yours."

"What's wrong now, Perkins?"

"Well, sir, nineteen books on our newest publication
list are going like hotcakes. *Mad Desire in Polynesia* is
selling like crazy. *A Thousand and One Reckless Nights*
is heading for 300,000. But those punks on our editorial
board picked a flopperoo in *The Taming of the Shrew*.
That Englishman wrote it – *you* know – Shakespeare.
It's a dodo egg. Five hundred sales."

"Good grief, Perkins! Why on earth didn't you veto
them? You know as well as I do wild animal stories
went out ten years ago! *The Taming of the Shrew*! And
what have they got on the cover? A picture of the
shrew, I suppose!"

"Yes, sir, I – "

"Well, take it off! Put a picture of a woman on it! A
good-looker in a flimsy negligee, staring back horror-
stricken over her shoulder. Tell 'em to roll off 50,000
for a starter and see how it goes."

"Say, that sounds *good!*"

"And tell the artist to have the negligee slipping off the shoulder. Better make it 75,000."

"You're really perking, boss!"

"And show a bronzed man wearing a loincloth creeping in a back window with a knife in his teeth. And, oh yes, for heaven's sake don't forget the revolver lying on the floor, still smoking. And the negligee should be tattered enough to see her bosoms and upper hips, as if she has just been chased through the bramble bushes. Make it 100,000."

"Great, boss, great! Don't stop – I'm taking it down in shorthand."

"By gosh, Perkins, you're right – it *is* good! This book is getting more interesting all the time; it may hit a million! What did you say the name of it was? *How to Train Moles?*"

"*The Taming of the Shrew.*"

"Retitle it *Untamed Pagan Adventuress.*"

"Gee, boss – a sheer stroke of literary genius!"

"Thank you, Perkins. Well, see you later. I'm worn out and I'm heading to Florida for my winter vacation. And, by the way, tell that English writer friend of yours to stick along with us. We'll make him famous!"

Why I Like Not To Meet Freddie Smivett

I f there's any man I try to dodge past on a crowded sidewalk, it's Freddie Smivett.

Freddie never hits anybody when he's mad, but wishes he had the nerve to. So he compensates by vehemently describing to his friends how he almost hits everybody. Unfortunately, he works himself up to a loud pitch.

He catches me slipping by, seizes my arm, and immediately remembers his dispute with Mr. Needham, the butcher.

"So he asks me," says Freddie hotly, "why don't I eat fish then, and I says, 'I'D JUST AS SOON PUNCH YOU IN THE SCHNOZ AS TALK TO YOU . . .' "

He grips my lapel and curls his lip to show how he said it. Passers-by slow their pace and watch us hopefully.

" '. . . YOU . . . DIRTY . . . RAT,' " he adds, through clenched teeth, keeping me fixed in his fierce gaze.

Several people are now standing a discreet distance away, shuddering pleasurably and waiting for the punch to land.

I don't like to look at his unnaturally contorted face, so I nod agreement with whatever he is saying and glance casually at the store windows, leading spectators to think I am foolishly giving him a clear shot at my chin.

25

Jutting his jaw close to mine, Freddie continues, "I says, 'KNOW WHAT I THINK YOU ARE? SCUM . . . JUST SCUM.' "

To divert him to a more tranquil subject, I nod vigorously and ask quietly how his back-yard garden is coming.

"Oh, pretty good," he says, reluctant to stop intimidating Mr. Needham. Then he brightens as he remembers a disagreeable thought. "Mrs. Plotz threw more garbage over the fence near my radishes yesterday," he begins, his eyes narrowing, "and I points to her clothesline and says, 'YOU DO THAT AGAIN AND I'LL THROW MUD ON YOUR GOOD SILK NIGHTSHIRT!' "

This is terrible. I would rather be threatened with the punch on the schnoz than have people think it is my whimsical eccentricity to wear silk nightshirts.

"And," Freddie goes on, "guess what she says?" He wrinkles his nose and shrills at me in a high falsetto: " 'I HATE YOU. I HATE YOU.' "

This is too much. I suddenly get up courage and wave at nobody in the rear of the onlooking crowd and exclaim, "There's my wife waiting for me!" And, catching him off balance with surprise, I break away and disappear among the spectators, leaving him to look for someone else to almost punch.

And Par.
Can't Be Broken,
Except Into Sentences

Use of abbreviation
  Can hold down word inflation.

But my dictionary
  Seems contradictionary.

Pharm. is not to raise chickens on,
  Nor Sax. to raise the dickens on.

There's no peak in the Cap.;
  You can't speak to the Chap.

Def. doesn't mean Grandma, nor Lit. mean Grandpa,
  And Sec. is not what you are asked to wait just a.

Gal. is not intended to be kissed,
  Nor is a villain meant by Hist.

Dial. is phoneless, and Sing. is toneless,
  While Exclam. is not a former clam.

Imp. is not impish, nor is Syn. sinnish;
  M.E. is not me, it's Middle English.

It's all sort of confounding-like –
  It isn't what it's sounding like.

The Art of the
Compliment Gracious

A book on social etiquette, 1905, which I found practically good as new in an attic trunk, says: "In greeting the hostess, the guest will offer some chivalrous comment on her becoming appearance. Such niceties bespeak him as one of the gentle breeding."

I have tried this advice. It is all right as far as it goes. But it doesn't tell what to say to sound convincing to dowagers; and I can never seem to get away with what I think up myself.

For instance, I attend the canvassers' reception at the home of Mrs. J. Chiltenden Jones, the co-chairman of our community fund drive. With a new upswept hairdo and a new swept-up face, she gushes a welcome to the arriving guests, and one of the men remarks gracefully, "Why, Mrs. *Jones*! I thought you were one of your daughters."

She beams: "Flatterer!" and gives him a deprecating pat as she passes by.

Then I say, "Why, Mrs. *Jones*! Your hair is lovely. You look twenty years younger than when I saw you yesterday."

I wait for the playful pat, but instead she smiles sweetly. "And just how old would you say I am?"

She has me cornered, and she knows it. I don't dare make a guess; she would add twenty years and say so *that's* what she looked like yesterday.

"Oh, I'm no good at ages," I say quickly, with an un-

comfortable feeling I'm contradicting myself. Fortunately we are interrupted when a youthful-looking
man staggering under the weight of an armchair asks
her, "Where do you want this put, Mother?"

She waves him on, and I continue, trying to be buoy-
ant, "You know, Mrs. Jones, you really don't look much
older than your son."

"That," she replies, with the fixed smile never leaving
her face, "is my husband." Then she calls in a mock
petulant tone, "Henry! I want you to meet someone
who thinks I'm your mother. Yesterday I was your
grandmother."

Henry comes over reluctantly, with a wincing smile
that asks why did I have to start something so early in
the evening. I'm still standing with my coat on, turning
my hat inside out and back again and then crumpling it
nervously together.

"She's quite a joker, Mr. Jones," I laugh feebly. "Why,
your wife looks *years* younger than her portrait over
there. It catches her personality so well. Who painted
it?"

"An artist named Van Dolph," Mrs. Jones replies, still
smiling. "In 1806. He titled it, 'Dame Scraggs, the Last
of the Witches.' She was eighty-six when she died."

"They hanged her," Mr. Jones corrects reflectively.
"The legend is that she is born again in each generation."

Floundering helplessly now, I glance involuntarily at
Mrs. Jones and blurt, "Oh, I don't think there's anything in that."

Mr. Jones, following my lead, looks at her too, and
then, in the embarrassed silence, looks at the portrait
and shudders.

"Well," I stammer, "thank you, thanks for everything.
I've had a wonderful time, but I really must be going.
I'm keeping both of you up so late. Thanks again. Good
evening!" And I hurry out into the street, shutting the
door quickly.

Not until I get out do I remember, with a start, I was
going in. But perhaps they didn't notice it.

Diagnosis of an Antipathy

Dr. J. Schnuff McPhee,
  Who's skilled at surgery,
Has always known me
  And would gladly treat me free.

But he won't, by cracky;
  That man will never see
My tongue or vertebrae,
  With or without a fee.

I speak to him brusquely,
  And then walk on briskly;
He takes my rudery
  With some perplexity.

I think you'll agree
  I've acted sensibly;
You see, when I was three
  (And rather small for three),
That dirty-faced rowdy,
  That sniffy-nosed bully,
Toughy "Snuffy" McPhee
  (Who was quite big for three),
Well, to make it short, he
  Grabbed up all my marbles and said,
    "Try and get them";
I didn't; and, by God, I'll not soon forget them.

Just Keep Those Kids Out of My Sight

After a lifetime of struggling to stay young, I'm happy to say I've discovered at last the secret of how to do it: never look at other people's children.

It's as easy as that!

Other people's children have a very annoying habit, which I've noticed repeatedly, of sprouting up a foot or so every time I turn my back on them.

I can see no possible reason why they do it, except to make me feel older every time they're introduced to me. It's pure maliciousness, and it pretty well shows the respect that the present generation has for older folks' feelings.

"This is my little Woodley," says Mrs. Bleeker proudly when she calls on us. Towering above her in the doorway suddenly appears a grinning, freckled, toothy head, separated from a huge pair of shoes by six feet of clothing which covers, I can only think, an extension ladder. The apparition doesn't speak; it just grins.

I start involuntarily.

"Good heavens! *That* isn't little *Woodikins* – the boy who used to make mud pies on our steps!" She probably thinks I'm only being polite, but my despair is genuine.

"This is my baby, all right," she says with a lilting smile, reaching up to try to smooth the rumpled hair of the big orangutan. "You can't imagine how old I feel just to look at him!"

How old *she* feels? That's unimportant. She doesn't mean it anyway; she just wants to be told how young she looks. What bothers me is how old *I* feel. It's terribly upsetting. Surely it was only a few months ago that the Bleekers were living next door and I was wishing I could dump some mud on their steps, too, without being taken to court.

Perhaps it *was* a few years ago; yet I have an uneasy feeling that if I let her baby slip out of my mind again and don't keep watch on him, he'll be back next week with a moustache and a wife and three kids and will automatically make me feel another twelve years older. Give him a month on the loose and I'll be doddering.

That's why I've decided not to look at anybody's children from now on, except my own grandsons. Thank goodness the two of them, aged nineteen and seven, are very sensible – they never change. Some of my friends, I admit, are under the insistent delusion that the boys have been springing up like weeds, and seem quite worried about it, glancing anxiously at their receding hairlines in the mirror every time I introduce them.

But that's ridiculous. I'm quite certain my grandsons have always looked just about the same as they do at the moment, and I can't see why they should upset anybody.

Hilarious Interlude

This girl I'm watching on the phone
  Is surely not the wife I've known.

She's normally so serious –
  But now – just look – delirious!

She laughs, she gasps, she shrieks, she screams;
  Her friend's a dazzling wit, it seems.

Agog I sit, while her sides split,
  And try to guess the cause of it.

Then I ask, "What was so funny?
  I would like to laugh too, honey."

She looks at me with some surprise,
  And knits her brows and then replies:

"I can't imagine what you mean;
  Myrt just spoke of a hat she'd seen."

The Ruggedest Sport

"... and now McNulty's really going after Morrow – a right smash! A right hook! *Another* – and *another*! But Morrow comes back with a hard left jab to the ribs – and now a right uppercut by Morrow – *wham*! He rocked McNulty with that one – caught him flush under the jaw – you could hear the thud of the glove way up here in our booth! Now there's a clinch with the referee somewhere in the middle! Wow! Those boys won't stop throwing punches for a second! Look at *that*! Morrow tried a tremendous roundhouse right and missed McNulty's head – Morrow spins around – McNulty's really clobbering him – a right! – a left! – a right! – a left! Boy oh boy! Listen to the fans roar! The referee's trying desperately to stop the fight! The police are taking a hand – they've grabbed McNulty, but he's still swinging! Morrow's charging back at him now – the police have him, too! What a *fight*! The crowd is on its feet screaming for more! Those boys have put on the biggest and best boxing match the stadium has seen all year! Yes, sir – far more action than the Schrola-O'Hallorahan title bout that Schrola got $750,000 for. Now the referee has skated over to the penalty box, and it looks like they'll both get major penalties and perhaps hundred-dollar fines. They certainly should, too, because an unsportsmanlike exhibition like that is a disgrace to the name of hockey."

Membership Committee of the Retired Bankers' Chess Club Rejects a Candidate

Mr. Chairman: Our committee
   Feels it is an awful pity
That we have an application
   With a nasty complication.

It's from one of those new electronic
   Brains that play chess with speed supersonic
And solve all problems mathematical
   And find no problem problematical.

But, sir, it has occurred to us
   It would be quite incongruous
To let this synthesis play chess
   In our respected club, unless
Its sponsors work on it some more
   And teach the dratted thing to snore.

Licked Again

Or, 108 Days Becalmed in the
Post Office Stamp Wicket Line-up

I wish the girl ahead of me
  Would say for once, just once, "One 'three.' "

I've never had that luck; but gee,
  If I pray hard . . . just *possibly* . . .

She *said* it! But, heart-rendingly,

She said it this way: "Let me see – a hundred ones,
eighty-seven twos, fifty-five fives, forty-eight sevens,
sixty tens, five twenties, twelve thirty-twos, two
fifties, an airmail special-delivery postage for Singa-
pore, and registration for these six parcels going to
Khartoum. And, oh, I'll have to pay you in pennies
out of our Sunday school's piggy bank, and I'll need a
receipt of course. And – I almost forgot – one three."

Who Said This Is
the Age of Leisure?

S tatisticians say their investigations show that
people have more leisure time in the modern age
than ever before. This seems odd. They couldn't have
investigated the people I meet.

In good times or bad, my friends confide to me they
have never worked so hard. They are always killing
themselves, and want to be admired for it.

When I bump into a casual acquaintance and feel embarrassed because I can't remember his name, it is
always safe to notice he is killing himself. This makes
him so happy he can't think of anything else.

"Why, hello!" I exclaim. "Say! You look as if you're
working pretty hard these days."

He brightens immediately at the suggestion, and
slumps his shoulders to go with the role.

"Just pushing myself into the grave," he says grimly.
"How about you?"

"Oh, working every minute," I reply, so he won't
think I'm a poor sport who wants to stay alive. "But
you'd better take care; you'll kill yourself."

His eyes glisten with pleasure, and he shakes his
head defiantly. "Got to keep up the pace in times like
these, even if it does kill me."

"Shouldn't you see a doctor?"

He frowns irritably at this; I can see he is determined
to finish himself off as quickly as possible and resents

the idea of anyone butting in and trying to throw cold water on his plans.

"Doctors!" he says disdainfully. "They've thrown up their hands. They give me only two more years."

"They hold no hope?"

"None at all. They say I'd last thirty years if I took vacations, but that just shows how impractical doctors are." He laughs hollowly. "How do they think *I* can take vacations?"

"Pretty hard, in your business." I have no idea what his business is, but if I manage to pretend long enough he may go away.

"Haven't let myself take a vacation for four years," he says proudly. "It's just murder."

"You can't do anything about it?"

"Of course not. Last time our gross volume slipped 2 per cent in three weeks. Do those doctors think I'm crazy enough to do it again?"

We both enjoy a chuckle at the very thought.

"It's not the work, it's the nervous strain that's killing you," I remark hopefully, though it's probably too much to hope he will drop dead right now.

"That's it exactly," he says eagerly. "It's terrible in my business, as you say. I don't know how I keep so sane."

"It's the kind of people you have to deal with," I continue, desperately parrying for time. "They're so unreasonable."

"*Aren't* they!" he says gratefully. "Not many fellows appreciate it like you do. Why, you know as much about my business as I do myself."

"Oh, I wouldn't say that."

"Don't be modest. You're a born business analyst. You've sized up every problem I get and other businesses don't. How about dropping in at the office some day soon?"

"Great! I'll drop in."

"Don't forget, old pal; I'll call you up and remind you."

I'll never drop in, of course, because I don't want to and I don't know where he works, and can't even remember his name anyway. And he can't call me up, thank goodness, because I'm sure he doesn't remember me either.

Welcome, Neighbour!

As I am a very friendly person, I always like to make new neighbours feel welcome as soon as they arrive. Strangers appreciate somebody showing an interest in them.

When the Fiswells moved in next door last week I was right there, smiling and nodding repeatedly at them from my verandah as they directed the furniture movers. They just stared back; they still felt like strangers, you see.

After supper I saw Mr. Fiswell lying back in a lawn chair with his eyes shut. He seemed exhausted. I walked right over and said, "Having a little nap?" He looked startled, and said yes, he was.

The trick in making friends, you see, is always to ask something that calls for a yes answer. It starts everything off on an agreeable note.

Bright and early next morning I saw Mr. Fiswell through his open bathroom window. "Having a shave?" I asked, smiling. He seemed to be taken aback, and said yes, he was. I couldn't blame him for jumping; he wouldn't find such friendliness everywhere.

Taking every opportunity to make him feel at home, I asked him in the next few days:

"Doing some reading?"

"Washing the car?"

"Watering the garden?"

"Mowing the lawn?"

"Putting up the clothesline?"

"Eating an apple?"

"Thinking about something?"

"Not feeling so well?"

He said yes in every case, of course, but he seemed the kind who has a hard time making friends. In fact, he talked less and less. I think he had a problem on his mind.

When I passed the Fiswells' kitchen window on the fourth day, they seemed to be having quite a fracas. Mr. Fiswell was shouting, "I've had all I can stand of it, I tell you – it's worse than Chinese water torture."

To pour oil on the troubled waters, I looked in and said, smiling, "Having a friendly little argument?"

Mr. Fiswell wheeled around, wild-eyed, and said rather tensely, with his lower teeth showing, "Why, no – we're rehearsing for a play. Do you want to buy a ticket, or have you seen it all?"

"Why, certainly, thank you," I said. "I'll take one."

Oddly enough, Mr. Fiswell didn't bring me the ticket. I suppose he got so preoccupied with all the work of moving again yesterday – they couldn't have been satisfied with the house – that he completely forgot it.

Well, I see a furniture truck has just finished moving the McCullochs in – they're the new tenants – and there's a man out front, who must be Mr. McCulloch, raking the leaves. I must hurry right out and ask him if he's raking the leaves.

New Year's Mourning

I wish I could remember
  What I can't;
And wish I couldn't remember
  What I can.

The Cool Courage
of Phil Perkins

I envy Phil Perkins. He's brimful of confidence. Weaker spirits may falter, but he uplifts them. He's a great comfort in times of distress.

When our wives drive to Springvale with a group of women for the day and don't return by mid-evening, that is understandable to me. After all, Springvale is a hundred miles away. I don't even think about it.

But at ten PM the phone rings.

"Hello," says a man's voice. "This is Phil. Any sign of the girls yet?"

"Not a sign."

"Well, don't worry about them. They'll be all right."

"Oh, I'm not worrying, Phil."

"That's the stuff. Naturally if they met any trouble they'd have phoned us."

I go back to my book, but for some reason the characters don't seem to be getting anywhere, although I don't suppose I can expect them to if I never turn the page. It *is* quite late; they've never been this long before.

The phone rings, startling me.

"Hello," says Phil. "No word yet?"

"Not a word."

"Well, don't let it upset you. I was just thinking: if they had an accident the hospital or the police would let us know. Anyway, a smash-up doesn't always mean anyone gets killed. I've heard of people coming out of awful crashes without a scratch. If I hear anything I'll let you know."

I thank him, but despite his brave reassurances I can't settle down. I can only keep admiring the calm courage of Phil Perkins and wishing I was more like him. I light a cigarette, blow out the match, put the match in my mouth and throw the cigarette into the fireplace. Every time I look at the telephone I shudder.

Suddenly it rings, and I grab the receiver.

"Just something funny," Phil's voice says, "to cheer you up. I had a call from Harry Wilson – his wife's driving the car, you know – and guess what he's fretting about? The *car*. No kidding. He doesn't seem the least concerned that his Hilda may be lying out there unconscious; all he can think of is that '66 crate he just had repainted. If she goes and wrecks it and kills herself, he will be quite exasperated with her. Wouldn't that slay you?"

It almost does. Then Phil adds reprovingly, "We shouldn't be calling each other up like this; we may be interfering with long-distance trying to reach us. How about both of us agreeing to call only in case of bad news?"

I agree, numbly, and by now I feel that bad news is inevitable no matter how it comes. I pace up and down, take the dog out for a walk to kill time, but check myself when I get to the street because I can't hear the phone. So I come back, noticing I didn't have the dog on the end of the leash anyway.

The phone jangles, and I lunge for it feverishly.

"Hello," says the voice. "This is Phil." My heart pounds. "The car" – he clears his throat, and then blows his nose, which takes several minutes – "the car has just arrived at my house, and your wife will be right over; so you can see how silly you were, and we can call off that arrangement we made about phoning."

44

Ode to the Fall Job
of Cleaning
and Polishing
the Storm Windows

How is it that these streaks I'm trying to rub off,
  Every time,
Prove to be on the other side of the window
  From which I'm?

It's Tough
To Be a Burglar
These Days

I might as well admit it. I scared myself so badly,
thinking about killings, rapings, violent muggings,
and break-ins in Miami, that I went to a shopping mall
when we arrived in Seminole, Florida, and bought several sets of metal window-locks at $1.59 a set for our
condominium apartment. I was being extra careful
even though we lived on the other side of the state.

When bedtime came, I said to my wife, "Did you put
those things on the windows?"

"Yes."

I checked the front-room windows: good – both were
now blocked at a height no one could climb under.

"But our sliding glass door at the back," I said, puzzled, "and our bedroom windows. They're wide open.
You haven't got fasteners on them."

"I know," she said. "I want the air."

In other words: "Dear burglar, if you wish to come in, please enter by the back door or bedroom windows. We are sorry for any inconvenience we may have caused you by locking the front windows."

It reminded me of the twenty years we owned German shepherds as pets at home in Rothesay, New Brunswick – ten years one dog, ten years the next dog.

Conscientiously I always double-locked the front door – but I never went to the trouble of locking the kitchen door.

Because the dog always slept in the kitchen.

In fact, not very long ago it seemed that few people in New Brunswick bothered to lock their doors at all.

I well remember our first visit to the picturesque island of Grand Manan at the entrance of the Bay of Fundy. We stayed at the sedate, upright Marathon Hotel. The manageress showed us our room, explained how to open and shut the bulky cardboard accordion-type bathroom door. As she was starting to leave, I said laughingly, "There's only one thing you forgot – you didn't give us our room key!"

She looked surprised. "Oh, there aren't room keys. We don't have any. You just leave your camera and things. No one will touch them."

I found out later that practically no family on the island locked its doors – with the exception of the resident Canadian Customs man. Because his work had trained him to be suspicious of people, he always locked his door. But because he was also a hospitable Grand Mananer, he left the key in the lock in case anyone wanted to get in.

And I remember telling my sister in the mainland resort town of St. Andrews about our Grand Manan experience. I thought she would shake her head and exclaim incredulously: "Can you imagine that!" But she didn't react at all. She just looked at me and said:

"I don't lock my door either."

Several weeks later I found out why. We arrived at her door, rang the bell – no one home – and thought perhaps we should just walk in.

Almost immediately two neighbour ladies appeared on their back stoops, watching.

"I'm Nan's brother," I called out.

"How do we know for sure?" one answered.

"Because I look like her."

That's a remarkable thing about St. Andrews. It doesn't need professionals to come to town to mobilize an official "Neighbourhood Watch." The town already had a very good unofficial system.

In Florida, of course, though 99 per cent of the people are extremely friendly and helpful, we always have to think of that one per cent who are neither.

U.S. recessions may come and go, but one industry that's really booming is the production of home-security devices – from handguns to alarm systems to guard dogs.

Even dear old silver-haired ladies in Miami have been taking revolver instruction from tough ex-Marine sergeants – how to hold the weapon steady in both hands, sight along the barrel, and fire.

"But don't fire while the burglar is coming over your lawn," the teacher smilingly cautions the class. "Until then the guy's only a trespasser. Wait till he gets into your house. Then shoot him."

Of course, the crime rate is not such a problem in a suburban area like Seminole on the Gulf of Mexico side, where we spent a winter. In fact, we felt perfectly safe in our condominium of row housing on the highway because it had big entrance signs saying MISSION OAKS. This made us sound like priests, and priests have no money worth stealing.

Nevertheless, most households are warily vigilant.

In one home where I stayed overnight, the host said anxiously in the morning, "Wait! – slide down the stairs against the wall like I'm doing. I have to turn off the burglar device." While we slithered down sideways like two crabs, he kept himself flat against the wall all the way to the front door, where he clicked a switch on a little metal box.

"If you got in the path of that electronic beam," he explained in relief, "a police car would be here in no time."

In another place I visited while looking for an apartment, Mrs. McGrogan, the widowed lady of the house, had not only an electronic-beam gadget by the front door (which emitted a piercing siren scream if an intruder interrupted the invisible beam), but also multiple locks on the back door and windows – and, on her bedside table, something that looked like a hand-held pocket radio.

"You may have noticed the transmitter behind the big chair in the living room," she said. "If I hear a noise I can press this little button; the box flashes a 'help' signal up the control centre in New Jersey, and it's flashed back to the Seminole police department – all in a twinkling.

"My nephew – he's in electronics up north – became so concerned about my safety he insisted on installing the whole business," Mrs. McGrogan added. "But I keep it turned off. I never connect it."

"Why on earth don't you?"

She sighed and explained very sensibly: "Because if I did, and a burglar came in, and the sirens suddenly went off, the burglar would be all right, but I would have a heart attack and die."

I had wondered at first why I saw so many people in Florida exercising Doberman pinschers and German shepherds on leashes, but now I know.

Obviously a would-be burglar today, even if he's armed, runs quite a gauntlet: the risk of being gunned down by a sweet old grandmother – "Hit the floor or I'll blow you away" – or being immediately captured by the police, or throttled by a guard dog.

One Florida TV station featured a reformed burglar in a program to teach people how to act when they hear strange footsteps in the house at night.

"The most effective way," he said, "is to shout loudly from your bed, 'George, bring the gun! Adele, phone the police!' Then you'll hear a crash as the burglar dives out through your patio door."

And what about a guard dog? What kind of a big dog is best?

"I'd suggest a little dog," the ex-criminal replied. "They make a loud noise yapping, and they'll go up to the burglar and wet on his leg. Then all the police have to do is look for a man with a wet leg."

This was fascinating. I'd never heard of it before. For days afterward I stared at every man's legs on the street, but I didn't find one burglar.

How, I kept wondering, would the little dog know whether it was really a burglar, or just Uncle Herbert from Fredericton newly arrived in Florida and sneaking in to surprise the folks?

All I can say is it would be quite a surprise for a burglar. Or for Uncle Herbert.

Happy Discovery Made by a Tourist Cabin Occupant after Three Sleepless Hours

No wonder this spray gun's insecticide
  Can't subdue the mosquito song
That's chased me to the brink of suicide.

          I've just realized –

The blamed whining thing seems to come my way
  Only when the tires of a car
Take the sharp curve on the nearby highway.

It's a Moving Experience

In one of those newfangled mazes where customers finally get to the bank teller's counter by going up and down narrow walkways between velvet ropes, I'm the nimblest of them all.

Tellers marvel aloud at how fast I can walk sideways like a crab.

Isn't that amazing, at my age?

But my ability isn't natural. It comes from squeezing sideways all day among the movers' huge cartons that fill the rooms of our new smaller home in Hampton, twelve miles upriver from our previous house in Rothesay. It reminds me of First World War trenches.

I never guessed anyone could accumulate so much clutter in only thirty years – including airline suit cartons and garbage bags full of old manuscripts, clippings, magazines containing my stories, mementos of trips abroad, photo albums – altogether fifty-five containers, plus two large metal filing cabinets.

Surprisingly, everyone I meet who has moved made a similar discovery – and it didn't always take them thirty years. Wives all exclaim the same thing: "It's a traumatic experience. Never again!"

My wife had always criticized me for having so many boxes of what became known as "Daddy's junk."

"The whole trouble," she said, "is you toss things into dresser drawers. If you just stood them up properly in filing folders, you could get all the cartons into two cabinets."

I tried that. And when we finally moved from Rothesay last week, I had two full filing cabinets neatly rearranged – and the fifty-five bulging cartons.

Nevertheless I'd planned the whole move wisely. For instance, at fifty-five dollars an hour it must have cost me twenty dollars to have the moving crew pack and load so many cartons of books, old skates, milk bottles and other things left over from our lawn sale, and transport them from our garage and unload them again. (I'd have gladly accepted fifteen dollars for the whole lot; and I'll probably end up giving them away anyway, or paying to have them hauled to the dump.)

Also, I'd made a conscientious attempt to sort out bills to be paid, reference material and photos and books to take to Florida the next week, letters to be answered, my large appointment calendar, hundreds of assorted items.

But at the last minute, seeing it was hopeless to finish the task with the movers already on the way from Saint John, I shoved everything into any open carton that could take it.

When we wearily started to get settled in Hampton, after bringing several extra loads in our station wagon, we made a strange discovery:

We couldn't find things.

My wife and several relatives had systematically packed carton after carton with clothing, china, medicines, electrical appliances, toiletries, and the like, and labelled each one in heavy black ink.

But puzzling questions arose. Such as: which category does an egg cup come under?

As for myself, I couldn't find anything.

Where was last month's telephone bill? My address book with long-distance telephone numbers? My treasured appointment calendar?

That appointment calendar worried me most. I definitely remembered writing something in the November-second square. But what was it? Had I been invited to speak at an important luncheon? Was I supposed to meet some visiting celebrity in Saint John? How could I explain why I didn't show up?

After frantic ransacking, I eventually found the calendar. In the November-second square was printed: "Change oil in car."

Apart from being unable to find things, I now discovered that exhaustion had made me hopelessly absent-minded.

I would put down papers on a table, turn around – and they disappeared instantly.

All my bills and manuscripts mischievously moved around the house and hid themselves.

When I packed my briefcase with documents to take to town, my wife intervened: "First get those last things out of the station wagon."

Dutifully I did, then we got into the car and headed for Saint John.

After a few miles I realized we hadn't brought my briefcase.

Rather than turn back, I decided to try to get along without the documents. When we returned after lunch to Hampton, my first thought was to locate the briefcase.

My wife and I looked everywhere.

It had evaporated into thin air.

Once she emerged smiling from a storeroom, with her hands behind her back, and said:

"Guess what I found?"

"My briefcase?" – elatedly.

"No – our Hallowe'en candy – left over from last month!"

In the afternoon she said, "You're sure you didn't leave the briefcase on the roof of the car while you were carrying in the things from our other house?"

"Lord! You think I'm absolutely crazy?"

Just to please her, we started to drive slowly towards town on the same route.

"You watch the left-hand ditch and look ahead and drive carefully," I said, "and I'll watch the right-hand ditch."

We'd driven only about 200 yards along Kennebecasis River Road when she cried out, "There it is! On your side, sticking out of the tall grass beside the ditch!"

I'd missed it.

Naturally this made me angry, because she was supposed to be driving and looking out the left side. She had no business looking out my side too. I told her so. I was going to offer a two-dollar reward for recovery of the briefcase but, under the circumstances, I didn't give her anything.

Two bright spots, however:

(1) In the turmoil of packing we discovered dozens of old things we'd long forgotten, which will be great for the next yard sale – including a short-legged pair of real silk handmade button-up underwear drawers, 1898 style, that belonged to the father of a famous Saint John artist.

(2) As far as my worries about completely unpacking and then immediately repacking for Florida are concerned, a Fredericton doctor told me he moved five years ago and hasn't got unpacked yet. Apparently all men suffer from the same symptoms.

Always Keep a List for Packing the Car

O ne of the secrets of happy long-distance car travel is to jot down, well ahead of time, a complete list of what you want to take with you.

I've found this of great benefit.

Not once since I began keeping the long list several years ago have I forgotten anything – flashlight, raincoat, nose spray, can-opener, binoculars, whatever.

Of course, the system isn't entirely infallible.

Once in a while on arrival I discover we need something I couldn't have imagined before we left home.

Who'd ever have thought we'd be feverishly groping through our suitcases in the Florida holiday season for a match! After all, we're out of the oil-lamp era, we have no fireplace there, and both of us gave up smoking years ago.

Like so many other newly righteous people, we no longer bother to steal all the motel matches.

But now we were desperate for a match to light our Christmas table candles.

Finally I ventured outside our condominium, where several silver-haired men from the management committee were trying, with much loud swearing, to string lights on a three-storey-high live Norway pine in honour of Christmas.

"I don't smoke," the first man grumbled at me. "Try him."

"I don't smoke either," said the other, "but here, I have a matchbook that's nearly expired." He chuckled.

On the cover, in stark bold black letters:

HOOK
Funeral
Home
11110 – 70th Ave., No.,
Seminole, Fla.

It contained two final matches.

This revived us. It saved our Christmas preparations.

But the idea of a funeral parlour putting out matches intrigued my curiosity. Did they keep a trayful in the Slumber Room entrance hall? Did they hand out one to each departing mourner? Free, or did they charge a cent? Was any portent intended by the flames?

It stayed on my mind. In short, I was hooked.

So I phoned the Hook Funeral Home. A very nice young woman answered.

I explained I was only looking for some information.

But before I knew it I'd been told I could have the deceased removed from the place of death to the funeral home for only $35. If I desired cremation, that would be only $125. A burial service would be in excess of $500, "the exact amount depending on how much previewing of the deceased you request."

Eventually I got the point across that I just wanted to ask about the matchbooks. The young lady laughed: "We're getting quite famous for our matches."

"How do you distribute them?"

"Oh, we have a boxful here. But we gladly send out shipments, on request, to condominium bridge clubs."

No wonder duplicate bridge players always look so serious.

I suppose I have no alternative but to give my wife some credit for being able to remember things that I just may have forgotten in preparing our Don't-Forget list for packing:

One November when we planned a trip to Florida, she had just undergone a shoulder operation and couldn't drive. I had been ill and couldn't either.

By great good luck a neighbour, Wilbur, a retired businessman, spoke up.

"I've never been to Florida," he said, "and I'd like to know the route. So if you'll pay my airfare back, I'll be glad to drive you."

Wasn't that wonderful?

It was, for the first day, even though I was wedged in the back seat so tight that my left arm was half held up by luggage.

On the second morning I began to feel nauseated. When Wilbur went into a service station to freshen up, I gasped to my wife, up front, "I'm terribly sick!"

"Why are you sick?"

"The awful odour! I can't take three more days of it – I'll have to go to a hospital."

"What's causing the odour?" – in puzzlement. "I don't notice it."

I lowered my voice. "It's Wilbur. He's sweating like a horse. He's all keyed up about driving us on this long trip for the first time. Lord, I'm sick."

She said, "Just a minute." Getting out of the front seat, she used her good arm to rummage into the piled-up baggage jamming me into the back seat.

Lo, she hauled out a huge heavy parcel. For some reason, the odour from the absent Wilbur now seemed overpowering.

"Our old New Brunswick cheese," she sighed. "The sixteen pounds I kept in the cellar for two years. I didn't think I could fit it into the trunk. But I imagined it was all right because it's wrapped in several layers of plastic and brown paper."

I'd completely forgotten we intended to take with us this last half-wheel of aged cheese made in the Belle-isle Creek cheese factory before compulsory pasteurization regulations forced it to close. Once there were nearly sixty such factories in New Brunswick; now none. This would have been a sad disappointment to Lord Beaverbrook if he were still living, because he often sent a shipment of the coveted extra-nippy Belle-isle Creek cheese to Churchill during the Second World War.

What a relief it was when my wife came back and announced she had somehow got the cheese squeezed into the trunk!

We were still laughing about it when Wilbur emerged from the service station. I told him the whole story.

He didn't laugh.

"I noticed it too," he said, frowning. "But I thought it was you."

Peculiar Phenomenon
Noticed in the
Blueberry-Picking Season

When my pail is full and it's too late to pick –
Why is it just then that I see where they're thick?

Save Future Antiques– Make a Million!

It doesn't do much good after all these years, I suppose, to reflect that if I'd had the foresight to buy a couple of dozen old automobiles off junk-heaps when I was in my twenties – Paiges, Marmons, Reos, Bristols, Chandlers, Willys-Knights – I'd now have a collection worth about one million dollars.

All for a total investment of fifty dollars or less!

But that's the story of my life.

I'm always saving things – but that seems to put a jinx on them.

Remember the Canadian twenty-five-cent piece with the picture of a Mountie on horseback that came out in 1973 to mark the RCMP's hundredth anniversary?

I bought thirty dollars worth of them, because I knew they'd soon go up in value.

They didn't. A million other Canadians had the same

idea. So one summer I took them all to the bank, after seven years, and got my money back.

The same with the 1967 Centennial dollar bills. I had twenty-six. They gained very little in value. I sold them too.

But in Florida I struck a real find.

Stores were selling off six-packs of Billy Beer – each tin bearing a rhapsodic endorsement signed by President Carter's unpredictable brother.

Apparently no one wanted it.

A customer sidled up behind me and whispered in my ear, "You planning to drink that stuff?"

"I haven't decided," I said.

"Well, fer gossakes, don't! It tastes like it was run through the stable floor first."

Nevertheless I bought a six-pack as a novelty at the distress price of $1.67.

"Better buy more," the store manager wheedled. "They'll soon be a collector's item."

Naturally I responded with a good laugh. I wasn't a fool. It was obvious that if every American thought the same way, a million people would be loading up with Billy Beer and soon it wouldn't be worth anything.

So I brought my lone six-pack home to New Brunswick and gave it away.

Next winter I was walking past the same store and I saw a sign in the window: HAVE A SHOT AT J. R. EWING.

Curious, I found they were offering a beer "Imported from Texas" labelled "J. R. Ewing's Private Stock" – named after the less-than-lovable *Dallas* TV character who had been gunned down that spring. The price was $2.79 for a six-pack.

On each can was printed: "If You Have To Ask How Much My Beer Costs, You Probably Can't Afford It. (signed) J. R. Ewing."

"You should buy some," the store manager advised confidentially. "It won't be on the market forever. Someday it will be a collector's item."

"Oh, I've been through all that," I said smiling. "I

bought some Billy Beer last spring. I imagine it's pretty well gone by now."

"Pretty well gone?" he ejaculated. "Pretty well gone? How much did you buy? Have you got any?"

"No. I bought a six-pack and gave it away."

His face fell.

"I can get you six dollars a can for it today – thirty-six for a six-pack."

I couldn't believe it.

Later that day I asked another man, who runs a package store at Madeira Beach, "How much is Billy Beer worth today?"

"Six dollars a can," he replied matter-of-factly. "I saw a can offered for sale at that price only yesterday."

"In a liquor store?"

"No, in an antique shop."

When I returned to New Brunswick, I hurried to the brewer to whom I had given the Billy Beer six-pack in the hope it was now an unusual display piece in his office. Did he still have the cans?

"No," he replied. "I ran them all through our quality-testing apparatus. It was pretty poor beer."

On my next visit to Florida, six months later, I discovered Billy Beer was now selling for $300 a can.

Some months later I saw a newspaper picture of a man in the U.S. Midwest, proudly standing behind three cans of the rare brew lined up on a table. He was prepared to let them go, he said, at $3,000 apiece.

And when the Superbowl football classic came to Tampa, and stadium tickets were as hard to come by as angel's feathers – even on the black market at $500 each – a man blandly advertised an exchange offer: his own prized can of Billy Beer for two tickets.

Well, I'm going down to the basement now to look around, as I see that today's dealers in collectibles are buying almost anything old – even the sterling silver Mickey Mouse ring of the 1930's ($300), Tom Mix championship belt buckle ($40), Shirley Temple 1936 movie poster for *The Stowaway* ($450), Dixie cup one-cent vending machine ($600), Franklin Roosevelt 1920 campaign button ($30,000), Mickey Mouse animated character clock from the 1930's ($600), Buck Rogers disintegrator ($435), Christmas tree Betty Boop light bulb ($70), Eversharp lady's pencil, 14K, engraved ($495), Mickey Mouse tumbling toy ($185).

Isn't that great?

But – oh lord! – didn't we clean out the cellar just last week for junk that brought an average of five cents an item in our yard sale?

How To Forecast
the Weather

M r. Tompkins, I see you are applying to be one of our TV weather analysts."

"That's right, sir."

"Let's hear you give a forecast."

"You mean today's weather, sir? Gosh, I don't know anything about it."

"I just want to hear your speaking voice."

"Well, ahem – a high-pressure system is pushing up from New England, promising to drive our prolonged wet spell out into the Atlantic. Chance of rain today: 50 per cent. Temperatures will rise to 68° to 70°F. Long-range outlook: sunny skies for the next five days."

"Very good! Now, what do you say half an hour later?"

"The high-pressure front coming up from the south has taken a turn to the west. This indicates our skies will remain cloudy for at least two more days. Chance of precipitation tonight 60 to 70 per cent, and 80 to 90 per cent for the following four days."

"Excellent! And now what do you say an hour afterward?"

"Good news for lovers of the outdoors! The fog has lifted, clouds are gone, the sun is shining everywhere in our forecast area. This is due to a strong movement of warm air from Ontario eastward. Temperature is 94°, chance of showers zero. Look for clear skies until next weekend."

"Great! In fact, that's practically the forecast I'm holding in my hand – the one we're giving this very minute! How did you do it? Have you rheumatism in your big toe?"

"No, sir."

"Were you holding a wet finger out that window while I was looking down at the forecast?"

"No, sir."

"It beats all. You've given me three very acceptable weather predictions in a row. One last question: what do you say half an hour later?"

"I go back to the first forecast, sir, and start all over again."

"Bully for you! Catch 'em before they have their picnic baskets packed. That's the idea – keep 'em listening! You're hired."

"Thank you, sir. But I have one last question. How do we know what the weather will be like five days from now when we can't say what it will be like tonight?"

"Oh, we'll teach you those fine points as you go along. Well, see you at nine AM tomorrow. Have a nice day!"

"Yes, sir, if it doesn't rain."

I Wish I'd Remembered to Brush My Teeth Regularly Five Times a Day

The firm resolves I quickly make
When my teeth begin to ache
Would make the dentist less extractive
If I could make them retroactive.

Please Don't Give Me
Your Kitten
To Look After

I love animals. Everybody knows it. That's the trouble. Friends think nothing of bringing a fluffy kitten to the house and saying, "We're going on vacation for three weeks and leaving Patches with you. You'll love her – she's a dear!"

They're right. Inside the house Patches is overwhelmingly affectionate. She purrs, leaps up on my knee when I'm reading, rubs her head against my cheek, curls up and goes to sleep under my chin.

But outdoors! Can this be the same kitten?

If I'm trying to bring her in for the evening, she knows it.

She pretends she's a rabbit and I'm the fox.

I get as close as three inches while her eyes study my every move – then, *zip!* she disappears into the shrubbery bordering the driveway.

If I stand there forever, no kitten will appear. But if I'm lucky, I can finally espy two beady eyes silently watching me through the daffodils.

Of course, Patches is in no danger as long as she prowls her familiar haunts in the side shrubbery and the backwoods.

But one day she discovers there's a traffic thoroughfare far down the driveway. She sees children laughing and talking loudly, walking by on the sidewalk – so naturally a kitten that's crazy about youngsters will gallop down and start to follow them.

I gallop down too, breathlessly, because cars and trucks are swooshing past in an endless stream – and to my relief a little girl picks up Patches and hands her to me.

That starts it. Every morning, when I let her out before breakfast, Patches hastens down the driveway to look for the children.

Finding none, she discovers there are fluttering birds and twinkling butterflies in the bushes across the highway, just waiting to be chased. So she darts across through traffic, with me in my pyjamas and dressing gown only a few feet behind her.

A passing woman shouts from the sidewalk: "Your kitten is going to be run over!"

That's a great help. What does she think I'm doing stumbling through the shrubbery? Chasing the butterflies?

Finally a sympathetic young woman comes over and shows me how easily it is done.

"Here, pretty kitty, kitty, kitty!" she chirps, extending a hand. Patches lets the lady's fingers almost touch her nose, and – *swish* – she's gone. So the young woman snaps a branch off a bush, with another branch making a hook on the end of it, and holds it down in front of the kitten. Patches thinks she's playing cat and mouse, and pounces on the stick. Expertly the young woman hooks the kitten by its flea collar.

By this time, a middle-aged couple walking past on the sidewalk keep staring across the road.

What is the man in his pyjamas doing lunging around in the bushes after the young woman? I only wish they thought I'm chasing butterflies; I know what they're thinking.

After she has been kept in the house, to make Patches realize she musn't go near the main road, I let her out again next morning, and she starts up toward the backwoods.

Half an hour later, no sign of her. Fearful she may be on the highway, I hurry down to see – and my wife's voice calls out: "You're only making it worse. She thinks it's a game – she's right behind you!"

Too adroit now to be headed off, Patches races past me, tapping my leg, and dives into our driveway bushes. It's up to me to make the next move in our game of tag.

On an inspiration, I sprint back to the house and pick up a little battery-powered burglar alarm we used in Florida. Then, from the sidewalk, I charge back up into the bushes, turning on the loud siren alarm, shouting, throwing gravel in her direction.

Patches scampers homeward up the driveway with me in pursuit, the alarm in my hand screaming while I hurl handfuls of gravel.

I observe the aging couple, walking homeward, staring again. They're seeing the same man in his pyjamas wildly chasing a burglar now, and throwing gravel at him while holding a raucous burglar alarm.

But where's the burglar?

Next time the alarm doesn't cause Patches to blink an eye. She knows it's harmless.

In desperation I bark at her – not a playful *yap-yap-yap*, you understand, but the full-throated deep bark of a huge fierce Newfoundland.

Up the driveway she bolts; I run after her, baying like a hound that has scented his prey.

This time the decrepit couple just stand at the end of the driveway, hypnotized at the spectacle of the man in pyjamas who, obviously hallucinating on something, thinks he has been changed into a dog.

That does it: I send the kitten back to its own quiet residential street – to a neighbour's home, where I'm happy to reflect there are children who love kittens.

But I notice that the old couple, for no reason whatsoever, now walk past our driveway on the opposite side of the road. Isn't that silly? It shows what advancing age can do: they don't even remember the sidewalk is on our side.

Thank Goodness That Yuletide Job's Done

Now that my cards have been mailed out at last
    To all those by whom I expect to be wished the same
       to,
I'd feel pretty good if I wasn't harassed
    By the vague thought there was one I didn't sign my
       name to.

Physically Phfft

Medical surveys report that people are healthier than ever. This is absurd. All my friends are sick. They may not look it, but don't let that fool you. Underneath their brave exteriors they are in bad shape. In particular, they always insist they are sicker than I am, which takes the fun out of being ill.

When I leave for the office after being laid up a week, I see Merville (Mervie) Briskett sprinting to overtake me at the bus stop.

"Well, well!" he says heartily. "How does it feel to be out again?"

He doesn't care how it feels. What he wants is a chance to say how bad *he* feels. It's up to me not to let him seize the initiative.

"Only fair, Mervie, old pal," I reply weakly. "Had a terrible cold."

"Head or chest?"

"Head," I say without thinking. The word is no sooner uttered than I realize he has caught my guard down. I have led with my nose.

"Why, you haven't had anything!" he says exultantly. "*I* had the worst chest cold Dr. Higgins ever treated, and" – bursting with pride – "I still have it."

"But you must remember," I interject, desperately trying to get in a blow for my nose, "I ran a temperature of 103.5."

He guffaws uproariously: "Say! If *mine* would only drop that low I wouldn't worry. I run a temperature *all* the time."

I see my bus coming now; I have to kill myself off quick or admit defeat.

"You may be interested to know, Merville Briskett," I say testily, "they think I had a touch of pleurisy too."

With this I triumphantly step into the bus, but before the door can close behind me I hear a shout: "A *touch* of pleurisy. Good heavens, you don't know when you're well off. I have *acute* pleurisy right now!"

I hurry to a seat by an open window; as the bus passes him, I take him unawares by saying in his face, "My doctor had to call in a specialist." Then I shut the window with grim satisfaction.

When I get to the office, the switchboard operator says, "I have a message for you from some man. He just called to tell you he had three doctors."

This makes me furious. "Get him back on the phone!" I explode. "Merville Briskett, at Mammoth Manufacturing. Tell him I had three too." (I did, counting the first one, who couldn't come.)

A minute later she rings my desk: "Sorry, but his office says he has just left on a business trip and will be out of town for three weeks."

That's what I call a very mean trick, and I'm going to tell Briskett so if he lives long enough to come back.

A Blessed
Day of Rest

H ow lucky they were on New Brunswick farms at
Christmas-time a generation ago!

"Nobody worked on that day," my wife recalled with
misty nostalgia in her eyes. "It was a day of rest."

This puzzled me, a city-bred boy who had to undergo
the hard work of being awake in bed for two or three
hours, just wondering and worrying, before they let us
youngsters rush downstairs to open our presents under the tree.

"Didn't your father have cattle on the farm at Cover-
dale?" I asked.

"Yes, forty Jersey cows."

"Didn't they get fed on Christmas?"

"Oh, yes, we older children helped Dad."

"You mean, like after Christmas dinner?"

"No, silly – in the early morning, before daylight. On
school days we could   sleep in till six-thirty. But on
Christmas we got up at five, because the hired man was
usually off.

"We lighted lanterns to take, and sometimes we had
to shovel snow to get to the barn and to the outhouse.
Often, if it was below zero, we had to make a torch out
of burlap wrapped around a heavy stick, soaked in
kerosene, to thaw out the hand-pump in the back yard
so we could get water for the livestock.

"After feeding the cows in the barn, we milked them

by hand, and separated the cream from the milk in the farmhouse. You turned the handle of the separator and had to reach a certain speed to make it work. Then the cows were let out in the barnyard and water was pumped into a tub for them."

I said, "That was all you did?"

"Yes, except naturally we had to feed the horses, the pigs, the hens and ducks too, and the silver foxes."

For some reason I was beginning to tire out just listening.

"And finally you went back to the house."

"First we carried in wood for the kitchen stove and furnace, if we hadn't got enough in already."

"And then" – wearily – "back to bed?"

"Oh, it was too late to go to bed. So we opened our presents and played with our toys, and had breakfast. And then in mid-afternoon, of course, we started the chores all over again, feeding, milking, and watering."

"But nobody worked on Christmas?"

"No – it was a day of rest."

Florida?
You'll Just Love It!

I must be a natural-born salesman. I just start telling people about my vacation in Florida and they assure me I've convinced them. They beg me not to say another word or I'll spoil the surprise for them. It's amazing.

Why, I only barely mentioned it to Percy Pincombe walking along Princess Street, and look what happened.

"I'd like to go," he said, "but of course I'm tied to a job –"

"Oh, you'll love Florida!" I said. "I can give you some tips. Now the best route to take – lend me your pen; I'll sketch it on your newspaper –"

"But I'm not –"

"Wait," I exclaimed, fishing in my pockets. "I've got a list of places to stay. Better write today; they go quick –"

"Thanks, some other time. Please don't bother." He seemed restless about something. "Well, here's the post office; I need stamps. So long!"

He was so preoccupied that he walked straight through the lobby towards the rear exit without pausing. He jumped when he heard my voice right behind him.

"And are oranges cheap! I ate three every breakfast."

Percy stopped suddenly and bought a stamp. Then he

kept going. I hop-skipped into step in case there was anything else he wanted to know.

"I memorized every day's temperatures, too. New Year's Day –"

Something was bothering Herb all right. He acted strangely. He said, "You don't need a haircut or a shave, do you?"

"No."

"Well, I do. Here's the barbershop. So long!"

When I spoke from the shoeshine stand in the corner a minute later, Percy was so surprised and pleased he almost knocked the razor out of the barber's hand. It's always fun to have a friend to talk with in the barbershop.

"I've got two hours of swell movies of the kids at Okeebenogee Keys," I said. "How about coming for supper?"

I could tell the razor was dull. Percy looked agonized.

"Thanks," he said, squirming, "but Enid's expecting me home –"

"I'll phone her right now. Boy, is it a laugh when I run all the movies again backwards – the kids dive *out* of the pool, ha, ha!"

Percy's face was covered with towels. I could hear him cussing. Barbers always make the towels too hot.

That evening was an experience he'll never forget. He told me so when he left at midnight. He'd never been through anything like it. It made him wish he'd gone to Florida a week ago.

Next morning I phoned his office: "Say! Enid hasn't seen the pictures. How about bringing her tonight?"

"I – I can't." He seemed to choke over the words. "We're – we're leaving for Florida – yes, today. Thanks anyway!" I realized he was choking with pure joy.

It's odd. I still keep imagining I see Percy in the distance uptown, but he vanishes. I see lights in his house, but no one answers the phone; he must have sublet the place to a deaf old couple. When I phoned his office to make sure he'd got away, they asked who was speaking before they said he was in Florida. You never know; even an apparently respectable fellow like Percy may be trying to keep bill collectors from finding out where he is.

How Do My Friends Always Know I've Arrived?

O ne of the amazing phenomena of Florida is that our phone starts ringing the moment we arrive from Canada and start unpacking the car at our Largo apartment.

It always makes me wonder: how on earth do our friends know we've just got here?

"I'll bet," I tell my wife at the first ring, "somebody wants to ask us to dinner – that's certainly thoughtful of them."

She rushes to lift the receiver. A man's cheery voice says:

"Welcome back to Florida!"

In eager anticipation she asks, "Who's calling?" He replies, "The telephone company. We reactivated your phone today and called to see if it's working all right."

"Oh yes, thank you."

"Have a pleasant evening."

I grab the next call myself.

"Sir, would you like to subscribe to our Medicare supplementary policy?"

"Thanks, but I have complete Medicare already, in Canada."

"Does it cover your medical and hospital costs in Florida?"

"Yes, with Blue Cross travel insurance."

That ends it.

Almost immediately the phone rings again. It's the Pinellas County Research Authority. She wants to know all the statistics about us, also whether we'd like to enter our name for "a free vacation."

I reply we've just arrived from Canada; this *is* our vacation.

Without let-up the calls keep coming.

My name, amazingly, has been drawn as the lucky winner of a free photo portrait, with a deep discount on extra copies.

Would we like to have high-quality meats delivered to our door, as many old folks are doing to save the strain of driving to the supermarket?

And – incredibly, in view of our supposed age – another voice breaks the glad news. We've won five free introductory lessons at the Arthur Murray Dance Studios!

Then a woman's anguished voice: "Oh, Father Ferenga, I've been trying to reach you but nobody answered the phone. I have to see you right away!"

"But I'm not Father Ferenga."

"Are you serious? You sound exactly like him. Is your number 595-5458?"

"Yes, but – ''

"Please, Father, this is a terrible crisis in my married life."

For a moment, as my wife is out getting a hairdo, I'm tempted to suggest she come around quick so I can hear all the details. But then I hear my wife coming in.

Next time I'm luckier. The young woman on the phone is obviously someone I've met before.

"Hello, Mr. Trueman! This is Diane."

Now, I know several Dianes, and I can never remember people's identities anyway, so I play it safe and say "Oh yes, Diane! How are you?"

"Great! Could I interest you in reserving accommodation at Serenity Gardens?"

I assume this is the nearby complex of homes for the very elderly retired.

"Really, I don't think so. My wife and I visited the gardens two years ago, and we found it rather too quiet for us."

"Too quiet?" – almost in disbelief.

"Yes. And the accommodation we saw was on the first level, with two levels above us, but it's pretty dark down there for us to stay in."

"Are you sure you're thinking of Serenity Gardens?"

"Yes – just past Seminole Mall."

"That's Seminole Gardens. I'm speaking of Serenity Gardens."

"No, thanks just the same."

A few days later I happen to see Serenity Gardens on a visit to George Sturgeon's rose gardens at Anona – the vastest display of roses in Florida.

It's a beautiful cemetery of its kind, Serenity Memorial Gardens, with no standing monuments except occasional embellishments like cherubs and angels, and with a flat bronze plate on each grave.

But I imagine it *is* pretty dark down there.

The Shoddy Mirrors
They Sell these Days

Those of us who can remember away back half a century and more, when quality meant quality, are dismayed by the products turned out by manufacturers today.

There's no comparison.

For instance, those full-length three-panel mirrors in clothing stores that show you how your suit fits from all angles.

I remember when they were excellent mirrors all the way around.

What do I find today?

The long mirror facing me is as good as ever. But the two side panels are cheaply made; they present a distorted likeness of the customer, almost like an amusement-park laughing mirror.

I hardly recognize myself.

Who is this man with a receding chin, badly sloping shoulders, and a bustle you could park a teacup and saucer on?

If anyone really looked like that surely he'd have sense enough to grow a beard and hide the chin.

And my hair! It appears to flow backward like a concert violinist or Lord Hoare in the British Parliament. I've never looked like that.

When I arrive home and tell my wife, it only proves again she enjoys seeing me discomfited. She insists there's nothing wrong with the mirrors!

"I've told you a thousand times to stand up straight. But you won't listen."

That's why I appreciate my neighbour Herb Frobisher. I went to school with him, and he's completely frank with me, as I am with him.

"I've noticed those mirrors myself," he says. "The side panels make me out to have the worst potbelly you ever saw."

"Well, you may have just a little," I acknowledge. "I've seen worse, though, like Orson Welles. But what about my buttocks? Do they really stick out?"

He studies me sideways for a moment.

"No more than they ever did."

There you are!

How devilishly clever today's manufacturers are! They make the crummiest of side mirrors because they can get away with it, knowing you'll think that's how you look now because you buy a suit only every six years.

"That's right," Herb says. "They try to shame you. If you complain to the clerk, he just shrugs it off: 'The mirror shows only what it sees.'"

"But I suppose you can't really blame the manufacturers," I admit. "In these inflationary times they have to cut corners to keep competitive."

"And to stay in business."

Herb, who has become quite distinguished-looking lately with his silvery hair combed in bangs like a

Roman senator, adds: "The stores are using cheap light bulbs, too. They make grey hair look almost white."

Then his face darkens. "And I don't know why they have to chisel us good-sized men all the time. If I want a pair of pants bigger than a forty-six, do you know they make me pay extra?"

"Terrible."

"Yes, and I'm only a fifty-two."

He looks down at his waist.

"There's another example! They don't put enough holes in a leather belt. Look. See? I had to punch out two extra holes myself."

I shake my head in disbelief. "I suppose it costs them two cents a hole, and – wait till I get my calculator – they save $10,000 on 500,000 belts."

"Twenty thousand for two holes," Herb corrects me. "They don't care if it takes me half an hour using roast-turkey skewers. That's a lot of work for no pay."

"Just start the holes with a skewer," I advise. "Finish them with the blunt point of one of those big knife-sharpeners. It takes me only a few minutes."

"Good idea," says Herb. "Thank heaven for another full-grown man."

Yours, Doctor,
As Ever

Dear Dr. Hipplewaite:
I was delighted to receive the book you sent me, *How To Cure Your Neurotic Tendencies*. It was very thoughtful of you to remember how interested I am in medical science.

At first the possibility crossed my mind you thought the book had some bearing on my own numerous ailments, but on second thought I could see how ridiculous this was. A neurotic, as I understand it, is a person who imagines things, and that has never been the case with me.

For instance, I recall the Saturday afternoon I had you paged on the golf links because I felt faint walking up a hill, with hot waves going up my spine, and you were good enough to walk the mile back to the clubhouse in the rain and advise me that as it was May I should take off my winter overcoat. There was nothing imaginary about that coat.

Then there was the fog in front of my eyes when I called you away from that salmon-fishing trip years ago. You remember what a good joke it was on me when you pointed out there was probably dust on my glasses, as I had been shaking down the furnace just before the attack came on. The dust, however, was real dust; it wasn't imaginary.

But the best joke of all, I know you'll agree, was

when I called you away from your honeymoon over my appendicitis attack. You recall it wasn't imaginary either. You found the cause of the trouble right away; I can't yet figure out how my belt got tightened the extra two notches.

So you can appreciate what a great time I've had reading the book about people who just *think* they have things wrong with them.

Well, there's nothing much new with me, doc, except we had a wonderful office picnic at The Spruces, seventy miles from town, yesterday. I must close now, but I'll be dropping in to see you Tuesday as I seem to have a peculiar numbness in my right knee. It might be a coincidence, but I wouldn't be surprised if it's the same baffling circulatory trouble that the newspapers are saying Prince Tokan of Yalania is coming to the U.S. to see about. I just can't understand it, because my knee felt fine when our book-keeper, Miss O'Brien, was sitting on it coming back from the picnic.

Yours, doctor, as ever,
Horace Middlemiss

P.S.: Please remind me Tuesday to ask you about that newly discovered fatal condition called transvalgenosis. I had never heard of it before, so I was very glad to read about it in your book because I'm positive I had a slight touch of it at the picnic after winning the pie-eating contest and coming second in the Hot-Dog Octoberfest. Also I would like to ask you about getting another copy of the book, as my wife has thoughtlessly mislaid mine and I cannot find it.

The Hospital Nurses
Are All After Me

Take a deep breath," said the nurse. Naturally I couldn't, because I was already holding my breath.

She punctured my bare buttock with a needle to inject a coagulant.

Said another nurse, "Take a deep breath." Again I couldn't.

She put a needle into my arm to get blood.

I always thought that if you're admitted only for a series of tests, a hospital is a nice place to go to get a complete rest and catch up on your reading.

The trouble was, they wouldn't let me. From the moment I rolled into bed, women in white kept coming into the room, armed with blood-pressure cuffs, thermometers, cardiogram machines, sets of scales, urinals, and especially those syringes tipped with needles.

Their favourite place to get blood was the inside

crook of my elbow. When one became well-pitted, they simply went to the other, humans having been foresightedly equipped with two arms.

The doctor came in and said with a frown, "Your blood is low."

No wonder. They'd taken it all.

I learned that whenever I expected a pill, it was a safe bet I'd get a needle.

When I remarked on the third day that all this lying in bed was binding me up inside, the doctor, who evidently had quite a sense of humour, laughed, "Just wait till you get your Epsom salts tomorrow night!"

I thought: well, a little Epsom salts might be just the thing.

The next evening a nurse appeared with a filled glass.

"Here's your Epsom salts," she smiled.

"Thank you," I said.

A short time afterward another nurse appeared:

"Here's your Epsom salts."

"No, thanks; I've had it."

"This is some more. I'll wait and take the glass."

I was watching the news on my seven-inch TV screen appended to the wall, just before bedtime, when another nurse walked in.

"Your Epsom salts."

"Gosh, I've already had it twice."

"So this makes three."

Fortunately, even though my hospital bed seemed higher than my own at home, and I was apprehensive about falling off it, I knew from experience not to ask the nurse to put the sides up. Because then you became a prisoner, unable to get out, as the control button for the sides is on the outside. So this was no place to be trapped, frantically groping to reach the cord with the call-button on the end, after three doses of Epsom salts.

In fact, it was three-thirty in the morning before I felt safe enough to try and snatch some sleep; but when I went out to the desk and asked if I could have a light sleeping pill, as I was due to be taken down below for a barium series at ten-thirty, I was told: "We don't issue sleeping pills after two AM."

At four AM I awoke, lying on my side in the dim light – conscious of somebody in white standing behind my back. Looking over my shoulder, I saw it was a nurse. In her hand she was holding a huge syringe.

"Would you move your behind over a bit, away from me, please?"

I wriggled over and got ready to pull down my pyjama pants.

"What are you going to do to me?"

"Nothing."

"What have you got in your hand?"

"A flashlight."

"Then why did you say 'Move your behind over a bit'?"

"You were going to fall out of bed."

Not at ten-thirty AM but at seven-forty-five AM an orderly came in pushing a wheelchair.

"Sorry to be fifteen minutes late," he said. "I'm going to take you down for your barium series."

"It seems like a lot of fuss, wheeling me down just to drink another milkshake container full of barium," I commented.

He looked at me.

"You don't drink it this time. You get it, as they say, 'where the sun don't shine.' "

Almost before I knew it, I was up on a slab-like table in the bowels of the hospital, surrounded by sophisticated radiological equipment.

"Now," the female aide explained to me, "you understand when you've taken the barium you have to wait about ten minutes while we take pictures. Can you do that?"

"No."

"Then we'd have to repeat the procedure."

"The same thing will happen again."

So they resorted to a "balloon" which they apparently filled with air to exert counter-pressure.

I'd been back in my room a short while when another orderly appeared. He carried tubing and what looked like a hot-water bottle. I dreaded what might be coming after such a stressful night and morning. This was getting painful.

"I'm here to give you a good cleaning-out," he said.

"Wait – I *am* cleaned out. Completely."

"This is to remove any trace of barium. It can harden like concrete, you know."

So the twelve days were too unpredictable, too full of surprises, for me to settle down and catch up with my reading.

Modesty had long since flown out the window – and so had any sensitivity on my part to the language I heard from patients who probably didn't know what they were saying. And I marvelled at how the nurses could cope with some messy problems and retain their equanimity.

One evening, as I padded by a darkened room where two old men were patients (I thought they were women, their voices were so high-pitched), I got this shrill greeting:

"When are you going to give us some heat, you goddamn son of a whore?"

I duly reported the request to the nearest nurse, who went in and turned up the thermostat.

"They're really nice old fellows," she remarked. "They both wet the bed. One admits it; the other insists there's a burst pipe in the brand-new hospital." She added with a sigh, "I said, 'There're a *lot* of burst pipes in this room.' "

Sometimes I joined the circle of old philosophers who hung around the sitting-room and solved all medical problems, present and future, with very little effort.

"Mark my words," one oldster in a striped robe was saying, "fifty years from now computers will be doing the operations. All these video terminals everywhere are running the hospital right now; if they say you get something, you get it; if they don't say so, you don't get it." We all agreed to wait fifty years and see.

Oddly, no one mentioned one great difference between the old and new hospitals – the absence of loud dish-clatter now in the carpeted halls. I remember, as a pneumonia patient in the old regional hospital, being scared stiff because I had only a narrow space within my chest wall to breathe, and if it narrowed further. . . .

Hour after hour I listened to the voices down the corridor for some possible clue as to how I really was. Mostly I heard only dishes, and orderlies making dates with the blue girls. All this time, unbeknownst to me, my wife had been trying to get me a private room because my cell-mate hawked and coughed all night. She finally succeeded, though she hadn't arrived yet to tell me the good news.

But the head nurse knew. And suddenly I heard the booming voice of Dr. Arthur Chesley saying to her: "Is Mr. Trueman in this wing?"

She answered, "Yes, in 534. But we don't think he'll be with us very long."

Came the welcome tidings on my twelfth day that the last examination procedure would have to be postponed until I got my blood count up by next spring.

"You can go home today, or perhaps better tomorrow," the doctor said.

I was elated, and I knew my wife would be, too.

You see, we had moved twelve miles from Rothesay up the Kennebecasis River to Hampton after thirty-five years, and the unpacking of fifty-five huge cartons had just begun when I was sent to the hospital. I was sure I had been a great help, even though my wife didn't think so, as I didn't know where anything should be put. On top of all that, we'd been trying to pick out things to repack to go to Florida.

Just a moment previously at the nurses' desk I had heard the floor secretary tell a man, "We're ready to discharge you, but your daughter refuses to look after you."

91

How lucky I was, I reflected, to have a gladsome welcome awaiting me.

I could hardly wait to phone my wife: "Today or, at the very latest, tomorrow!"

A silence followed. I thought that sudden happy emotion had choked up her throat.

Finally she said, in a flat voice: "Couldn't you stay there a couple more days?"

The lengths some women will go to just to hide their true feelings!

Our Fine
Literature Corner

I suspect that this anonymous verse, just possibly, will not attain the literary eminence of being called poetry. But older people relate to it – so much so that uncounted thousands have happily circulated faint sixth-carbon typewriter copies to their friends. Such personal impact is, to me, a measure of the success of verse on any level. I only wish I'd written it:

A Little Mixed Up

Just a line to say I'm living,
    That I am not among the dead.
Though I'm getting more forgetful
    And more mixed up in my head.

For sometimes I can't remember,
    Standing by the bottom stair,
If I must go up for something
    Or if I've just come down from there.

And before the fridge so often
    My poor mind is filled with doubt,
Have I just put food away
    Or have I come to take some out?

There are times when it is dark out,
  With my nightcap on my head
I don't know if I'm retiring
  Or just getting out of bed.

If it's my turn to write you,
  There's no need of getting sore,
I may think I have written
  And don't want to be a bore.

So remember I do love you
  And wish that you were here,
But now it's nearly mail time
  So I must say goodbye, my dear.

Then I stood beside the mailbox
  With my face so very red,
Instead of mailing you the letter,
  I opened it instead.

Thank heaven, even if I'm getting a little older myself,
I'm free of all these symptoms. I do occasionally notice
when I drop my incoming mail on the dining-room
table until I get time to read it, and come back from the
bathroom a moment later, *presto* – all the letters have
disappeared! Finally I find them beside the sink in the
bathroom. I always blame this on my wife's habit of
picking up things and rearranging them, although she
denies it.

   Once in our Florida apartment I discovered I had a
wad of Canadian dollar bills in my briefcase, left over
from trips around the Maritime provinces. I decided to
hide them where no burglar would possibly think of
looking. Next morning, unfortunately, due to the fact I
have so much on my mind, I couldn't remember where
I put them. My wife and I haven't found them yet. This
just shows, I think, I can outwit anybody.

Another verse of unknown origin which people past retirement age – at least, the men – delight in reading to one another, accompanied by great guffaws:

Old Is Beautiful

How do I know my youth is all spent?
　Well, my get-up-and-go has got up and went.
But in spite of it all, I'm able to grin
　When I think of where my get-up has been.

Old age is golden so I've heard said,
　But sometimes I wonder when I get into bed;
With my ear in a drawer and my teeth in a cup,
　My eyes on the table until I wake up.

As sleep dims my eyes I say to myself,
　Is there anything else I should lay on the shelf?
But I'm happy to say as I close the door
　My friends are the same, perhaps even more.

When I was young my slippers were red,
　I could kick my heels over my head.
When I grew older my slippers were blue,
　But I still could dance the whole night through.

Now I am old, my slippers are black,
　I walk to the store and puff my way back.
The reason I know my youth is all spent,
　Is my get-up-and-go has got up and went.

But I don't mind when I think with a grin
　Of all the grand places my get-up has been.
And since I've retired from Life's competition,
　My schedule's all scheduled (with complete
　　repetition).

I get up each morning and dust off my wits,
  Pick up the paper and read the obits.
If I see my name missing, I know I'm not dead,
  So I eat a good breakfast and go back to bed.

And another:

The Toper's Ode

The horse and mule live thirty years
  And nothing know of wines and beers;
The goat and sheep they also die
  And never tasted Scotch or rye;
The cow drinks water by the ton,
  At eighteen years is mostly done
Without the aid of rum or gin.
  The dog at fifteen cashes in,
The cat in milk and water soaks
  And then at twelve short years it croaks.
The modest, sober, bone-dry hen
  Lays eggs for nogs and dies at ten.
All animals are strictly dry,
  They sinless live and swiftly die
But sinful ginful rum-soaked men
  Survive to three score years and ten.
And some of us – a mighty few –
  Keep drinking till we're ninety-two.

And yet another:

The Vanity of Earthly Greatness

The tusks that clashed in mighty brawls
Of mastodons are now billiard balls.

The sword of Charlemagne the Just
Is ferrous oxide known as rust.
The grizzly bear with potent hug
Once feared by all, is now a rug.
Great Caesar's bust is on the shelf,
And I don't feel so good myself.

While on the subject of homely doggerel, here's a verse written early in the century by an aspiring poetess, apparently a spinster, and published in a nationally known U.S. newspaper. It makes you realize how far we've come from the Dolly Dewdrop essays of a generation ago. Everyone knows, of course, that a doodle is an unconscious sketch, often unintelligible, penned by someone whose mind is preoccupied with other things, like listening to an important speech or a long-distance phone call. Nevertheless this poem leaves me somewhat mystified, and vaguely uneasy:

If I Had a Doodle

I wish I had a puppy dog, a doodle, and a duck,
Tommy has a puppy dog, a spotted one called Puck.
I think I'd like a black one, or a foxy, or a poodle,
I know I'd like a puppy, but I would so love a
doodle.

I don't know what a doodle is, it might be big or
small,
It might have funny prickly feet, or have no feet at
all.
Perhaps it has no eyebrows, or it might be like a
snail,
But to be a proper doodle it must have a doodle
tail.

Eleanora has a duck, it's white, she calls it Duddles,
  It's very fond of eating worms and paddling in the
    puddles.
I know I'd like a baby duck, I'd like a puppy too,
  But most I'd like a doodle to do as doodles do.

Oh, if I had a doodle, I would mind it every day.
  I wouldn't say, "Now, Doodle, don't," when we went
    out to play.
How everyone would stand and stare when I took
    doodle out!
  Though perhaps there are no doodles, still they're
    nice to think about.

Of course, all the popular literary epics passed hand-to-
hand aren't in verse. Here's one that wives keep delightedly mailing to other wives:

Dear Friend:
  This chain letter was started by a woman like
yourself, in hopes of bringing relief to tired, dis-
contented women.
  Unlike most chain letters, this does not cost anything; all you need to do is send a copy of this letter to five friends who are equally tired, dis-
traught, and disgusted, then bundle up your
husband and send him to the woman whose name
is at the top of the list, and add your name to the
bottom of the list.
  When your name comes to the top of the list you
will receive 16,478 men – and some of them are
dandies.
  Have faith and don't break the chain; one
woman did and got her own son-of-a-bitch back.
      Sincerely,

      A Misunderstood and
      Discontented Wife

P.S. At the time of this writing, a friend of mine had received 186 men. They buried her yesterday, but it took three undertakers and thirty-six hours to remove the smile from her face.

How To Survive
a Yard Sale

Is your life full of nagging little worries?
What you need is a yard sale! It's great fun. Just plan the sale two weeks in advance, and in that short time all your old worries will disappear; you'll have too many new ones.

I know.

First: will it be a sunny day? Everyone in the family feels sure it won't be, because the long-range weather forecast is rain.

"Never mind – it will change four or five times," a sympathetic neighbour assures me. "You have to catch it on the bounce."

But now another subject of family debate arises: should prices be kept reasonably high, or very low to get rid of things? This causes ruffled feelings, because nobody can agree on any item.

Suddenly I discover my two old raincoats, one with a lining, being hung up to go into the sale.

"Great heavens," I exclaim. "Not my good raincoats!"

"You've got a brand new one – the light fawn one," my wife replies. "You don't need three."

"But" – in anguish – "what if I go deep-sea fishing someday, and the boat's seat is greasy? It would mark up my new coat!"

She's unmoved. "You've never been deep-sea fishing in your life. And you're not likely to go now."

Helplessly I watch as, one by one, my treasured articles of clothing are set aside for the sale. It does no good to rescue my coats, because my wife finds them again within moments after I hide them under the spare bed.

On Friday evening the weather forecast is "Ninety per cent chance of rain tonight; 30 per cent tomorrow."

Wonderfully, Saturday dawns bright and clear!

That worry is over. However, complete bafflement lies just ahead: why do people buy what they buy at a yard sale?

This is the Great Unsolved Mystery of the Ages.

No sooner had 9:45 AM come – five minutes ahead of time – than from the living-room window I see the waiting women surge past the ropes at the end of the driveway and hurry towards the filled tables.

"They're buying things!" a young granddaughter comes in to announce excitedly.

"What did they buy?"

"You remember that piece of purple rock I brought from Nova Scotia? The one I called a dinosaur tooth?"

"Yes."

"A man bought it for two cents."

In the next six hours I can only ponder:

Why is nobody taking any interest in our studio couch at twenty-five dollars, even after it's marked down to fifteen – when my neighbour at his table across our driveway has no trouble selling an old padded toilet seat with a rip in it? (We gave away the studio couch the next week.)

Why does nobody want a modern fireplace screen for fifteen dollars – one that we bought last year for twenty-nine – when our neighbour is successfully selling three battered old golf clubs? (In fact, one woman tells him, "I'll take a complete set if you have them.")

Why does a man offer our granddaughter five dollars for the old cigar box she's using to carry two dollars worth of silver change? (It's mahogany-coloured cardboard, but apparently he thinks it's real wood.)

Why do women scuffle over partly filled bottles of perfume at twenty-five cents? Or gladly pay a dollar or two for little plastic bags crammed with cuttings from sewing materials that my wife almost threw in the garbage?

And what do you do about people who want to dicker over every item?

But, our neighbour hurriedly informs me, haggling is as accepted a custom at yard sales as in buying a car or a house.

It seems to me that twenty-five cents is a very low price, to put it mildly, for each of two old tuxedo shirts, cleaned, still attached to the laundry's cardboard. But a man says without blinking an eye, "I'll give you twenty-five cents – if you throw in the other one too."

As the sale mercifully nears its end, my neighbour's thoughtful wife brings over a big trayful of egg and chicken sandwiches for the workers. When only three sandwiches are left, she suggests to my son, "Here – have one yourself and take a couple to your wife at her table."

He thrusts the tray through the crowd of women to his wife and says, "Here – you must be hungry."

Exclaims a woman, "Oh, thank you very much!" – and takes a sandwich.

"That's very nice," says another, taking a sandwich too.

My son stares down in disbelief at the one sandwich left.

"So thoughtful of you!" says a woman gladly – and grabs it fast.

Then a man's voice speaks up: "How much do you want for the tray?"

One consolation for me: no one bought my raincoats! Apparently they were too big. I got them back.

We took a big pile of women's clothing to Hestia House, a shelter for battered women and children.

They're very grateful for donations because most of the residents arrive with only what they're wearing.

And a heap of men's clothing went to the Salvation Army. To my dismay, when all the things were emptied out on the table, there were my topcoats! Not only that, but two pairs of my sports pants.

"You can't give away my good gabardine sports pants! I've hardly worn them yet."

"They must be thirty-five years old," my wife replied. "They're too small for you now."

"I can diet down to them!"

She just looked at me.

"Would you wear flies with buttons?"

"No."

That ended it.

When I told friends later about the button-equipped pants, my wife commented, "I didn't say *they* had buttons. I just asked you if you'd wear flies with buttons. But they did have pleats in front. Would you wear pants with pleats?"

"No."

A few days later, when we visited a tailor shop with some dry-cleaning, I laughingly related the whole incident to the tailor.

"So I almost ended up wearing pants with pleats."

He smiled, looking from one to the other of us to savour the full effect.

"Pleats," he said, "are coming back."

A Merry Christmas,
Stu,
To Muriel and You

For some reason, people's minds seem to run in the same direction when they make mistakes.

Every December I get one or two cards that say: "Hope you and Muriel have a wonderful Christmas."

That's nice, except my wife's name is Mildred.

She never says very much, but I don't think she likes the idea of me having such a wonderful Christmas every year with Muriel. Even though she has gradually become accustomed to it.

This past season, things got worse.

A Canadian doctor, who shall remain anonymous, wrote: "I hope you and Edna have a wonderful Christmas."

"Who's Edna?" my wife asked.

"I haven't the least idea," I said. "I don't know who Edna is. I don't know who Muriel is, I don't know who anybody is."

"Then why did he say Edna?" She was watching my face.

"Because," I said, "I can only guess, he's absent-minded. I wouldn't want him to operate on me."

That's the story of my life.

I try to be as reasonably well-behaved as the next man, but names keep popping up to haunt me.

Like the time years ago I got a bill from a prominent shoe store in Saint John.

It said: "Six pairs of silk stockings: $12.00."

My wife opened the bill.

She handed it coldly to me.

"Who got the stockings? I didn't!"

I could feel the crimson creeping into my ear lobes, even though I had no reason to feel guilty.

"I haven't any idea."

When I phoned the store they looked up their accounts. The young woman said: "Sorry. The bill should have gone to Trueman Buskins in Quispam. Just a small error."

"Yes," I sighed. "Thank you."

But that wasn't the worst.

The worst was the time I got a bill from the Saint John General Hospital years ago:

"Unpaid residue of account for Mae Trueman operation: $26.00."

My wife opened the envelope and abruptly thrust the bill at me.

"Who is Mae Trueman?"

"I haven't the slightest idea."

"Then why did you put her in the hospital? What's her real name?"

"I don't know, I just told you!" I said in panic, my ears and neck burning. "I don't know anything!"

She watched while I phoned the hospital accounts office.

"I can't make out the typing on the bill very well," said the young woman after a moment. "Is there a Mae Trueman in your family?"

"Lord, heavens, no!"

"Is there a Mac Trueman?"

"Yes, our younger son. He had his tonsils out six months ago."

"Was your account paid up at the time?"

"Yes, yes."

"You're right. I'm sorry – just a mistake in billing. A small error."

"Yes," I said. "It was."

Wives Just Can't Figure Things

There's no place like a fall fair for a man to give his wife a lesson in practical mathematics. Every new husband should do it as part of her household budget training.

"Here's the Karokian Club wheel," my wife exclaimed. "Let's win a blanket for a dime!"

This was my opportunity. "Notice," I said, "there are two hundred numbers. To be reasonably sure of getting a blanket, according to the law of averages, I would spend two hundred dimes, or twenty dollars. Right?"

"*You* probably would," she said, "but a woman wouldn't throw money away like that when she can get one at Birschfield's for $4.49."

"That's it exactly!" I said eagerly. "So why buy a ticket?"

"Because," she explained, "a blanket's a bargain for a dime. Can't you see that?"

I tried another approach. "Suppose there are two hundred horses in a race. You want to bet a dime."

"Isn't that too many horses for a track?"

"This is a big track. Two hundred horses, and no favourites. They all run just as fast as each other."

"They'd all finish together." She laughed, and then, thinking about it, shrieked hilariously.

"No, no," I said, annoyed. "One horse will win the race."

"How could it?" She started laughing all over again; this distracted me so much that I began to wonder, too, how it could. So I let her buy a ticket to see what I meant.

"What horse have I got?" she asked.

"What do you mean?"

"Well, did I pick a good one? I'd like to know."

Before I could reply, the wheel spun to a stop.

"Little lady over here!" the Karokians shouted, hurrying the blanket to my wife, who was expecting it anyway.

Quickly I pointed out, "See what I mean? Now, according to the law of averages, you might easily spend $19.90 worth of dimes and not win again."

I said nothing more, to let the lesson sink in, until on the way back through the midway she suggested suddenly, "Let's win another blanket; we need a pair!"

"Now look," I said. "Don't you know the chances are thousands, maybe millions, against picking a two-hundred-to-one shot twice?"

"All right then, so I'll just try once."

The wheel whirled.

"Little lady over here!" the Karokians shouted, rushing the blanket to my wife, who was expecting this one too.

So I gave up completely.

I didn't even think of these incidents again for years and years – until the other day.

My wife, I should mention, has an exceptional knack for finding things. When she walks across somebody's lawn, she invariably comes up with two or three four-leaf clovers. When we cross a parking lot to enter a shopping mall, like as not she'll pick up a ten-cent piece or a quarter off the pavement.

This week it was a quarter, and she remarked, "That makes sixty cents I've found lately. Why don't you put in forty more cents and we'll buy a lottery ticket for a dollar – I've never bought one before – and we'll share what we win."

Here we go again, I thought.

I tried to explain to her it was like throwing money away, that the chances were extremely slim, the total receipts had to be skimmed off to pay the ticket sellers, the officials in charge, the governments, and so on.

But I handed over the forty cents anyway, just to humour her, and she bought the ticket.

Next day, when we went back, she had won ten dollars.

I didn't say anything, except to mention she said we'd share the winnings.

"So could I have my five dollars now?" I asked.

Suddenly a remarkable understanding of mathematics came over her.

"You put in only forty cents," she replied. "That's 40 per cent. So here's your share – four dollars."

Well, I guess all my training has done some good.

The Problem
of Watching
a Big Ball Game

I'm tired of hearing old-timers talk about the harsh life they had to lead more than half a century ago.

They never had to face the really exhausting hardships of today – like trying to see a long-anticipated television program.

Before an important baseball game I take the phone off the hook without telling my wife, so no one can call.

It doesn't matter much. I should remember from painful experience that lots of other things can happen – and probably will:

1. The TV picture will start flipping over. Or turn blue. Or become a blinding snowstorm.

2. The electrical power will unexpectedly black out.

3. Peals of thunder will split the sky, causing my wife to exclaim, "Turn the set off quick – it may blow!"

4. The entire living-room carpet will have to be vacuumed immediately. "It can't wait any longer," my wife insists.

5. Our young nephew will suddenly say, "I have a terrible toothache!" It's my job to find a dentist and get him there, hoping the dentist will have a TV screen in the waiting room. Happily there *is* an illuminated screen. It's titled: "Follow These Next Five Steps to Healthier Teeth and Gums."

6. If it's a U.S. network, the first half of the game may be pre-empted without warning by a presidential

address to the nation – in which he will say the same things he said last week and the month before.

7. A woman neighbour in her nineties will invite us in for a cup of tea just at the game hour, and my wife will tell her, "Oh, yes, we'll be delighted."

She'll explain to me, "We can't offend her. She's old, you know. And she's never asked us before."

Well, I console myself, the old girl will tire out after ten minutes, and we can hurry home. But old girls don't, if they're lonely. We tire out first.

8. Astoundingly, when I tune in to my big baseball game, not one of these things happens. But something worse does.

In walks a bevy of the "girls," as my wife still calls them, mostly nurses she knew in training school.

"Oh, you're only watching television," one chortles. "We thought you might be busy."

They're bubbling with high spirits, full of gossip. All the prattle is so loud I can hardly hear what Billy Martin is yelling at the umpire's nose, even when I put my ear up to the TV.

"You should see Melissa's gown," one nurse is shrilling to the others. "Imagine – the cleavage actually goes past her diaphragm almost to her umbilicus! But the gown has darling little velvet-covered buttons in the back, all the way down to her coccyx."

Suddenly they become conscious of me sitting there, still doggedly trying to watch the game.

"Can't you turn that thing down?" my wife says, smiling because there is company present. "Here – I'll turn it off. That's better!"

I look in the next day's paper to see what Billy Martin said. The incident isn't mentioned at all. But I know it must have been pretty good.

My Friends
in Need

"He's in, all right – I can hear him breathing."

I don't know what's the matter with my sales resistance. Every fund-raising campaign seems to get me.

"I'm canvassing for the County Rifle Shooting Club," says the young man at the door. As I am not a rifle shooter, I'm about to tell him I'm not interested. But he continues eagerly. "It's very important to train good marksmen. You know what they say – 'A man's best friend is his rifle.' "

I can't deny it. I can see myself aiming a gun through covered-wagon wheel spokes at the Indians, and being unable to shoot it straight because I haven't contributed. I pay him.

A moment later another man shows up. "I'm soliciting donations for the Pet Preservation Society." I start to turn him down flat but he remarks, rolling his eyes

111

as sadly as a spaniel's, "You've heard the saying – how true it is! – 'A man's best friend is his dog.' "

Indeed I have, and it's very true. It breaks me down. I pay him, and almost go and get him a bone.

Then a purposeful-looking woman appears.

"I'm from the Mothers' Uplift League," she announces. "We're raising funds to send every mother a Mother's Day card so no one will be overlooked."

I'm just about to refuse when she picks a bit of lint off my coat, straightens my tie and reminds me quickly, "After all – 'A man's best friend is his mother.' "

After I wipe away a tear and blow my nose, watching her going down the path with my contribution, I see a man coming.

But I have had enough. I jump back, bolt the front door and start out the back.

"I represent," says a man who is at the back door, "the Local Pure Air Association. We're raising money to purify the air of the entire community next month with dextryl-2-ozone, the new wonder chemical."

"Thank you," I say firmly, "but I have already made my plans to die of impure air. I'm against everything; I won't give to anything."

Seeing I am absolutely inflexible, he starts to leave.

"One thing I *will* say for you," I call out appreciatively, "is at least you didn't try to tell me a man's best friend is his health."

He pauses in surprise and wheels around. "Say!" he exclaims. "That's very good – I'd never thought of it. It's very true, you know."

"I suppose it is." I feel rather proud of myself.

"Of course it is. You're quite right, sir. Is money more important? No. Is fame? No. A man's best friend is his health. Surely you can't refuse a dollar for your best friend."

It appears I can't. I pay him and thank him, and feel so healthy I expand my lungs with a deep breath of fresh air until I remember it isn't pure yet, so I blow it out again and remind myself not to breathe until next month.

Then I hurriedly fasten all the doors, close the shutters, put out the lights, and go to bed. They can say what they like, but the suspicion has dawned on me that man's best friend just may be the fellow who invented the door lock.

The Strange Case of My Love-Starved TV

I t was peculiar. Every time I sat down to watch the news on channel ten in Seminole, Florida, the picture on the little old black-and-white TV set started to flip over.

I endured this as long as I could, and then I got up with a sigh and walked over to change to another station.

But as soon as I got near the TV, the picture stopped flipping.

Thinking the television station must have been adjusting something, I returned to my chair, and sat down – and *flip, flip, flip,* the picture started doing it again.

It struck me after this happened several times that apparently I had fallen heir to a lonely-heart TV set. Evidently it was missing the owner of the house, who had been in Ontario since last April.

Another Ontario man, a neighbour a few doors away, told us he remembered having a TV back home years ago that was never happy unless he stayed right beside it.

In the next few days, to my surprise, I met half a dozen people, even a young woman bank teller, who had noticed this same moonstruck behaviour in their TVs.

But why were the sets behaving that way?

It made me wish I'd taken the time to acquire some elementary knowledge of things like radio, TV, plumbing, carpentry, electricity, and recreational language when I was growing up. I'm just not practical.

I'll never forget how awkward I felt years ago when a prominent Saint John merchant invited me to take a day's cruise on his yacht on the river. All the nautical terms were new to me. I didn't know, for instance, a rope on a ship may be called a painter. At a moment when the yacht was veering around wildly, the owner called to me: "Stu – grab the painter!" and I looked around quick for a man in white overalls to grab before he fell overboard.

It was the same experience when we moved into our Florida address in November. Many household fixtures, including the heating and air-conditioning system, refused to work. When I phoned the company that held the insurance policy on the system, a worried official asked, "Did you by any chance do anything to the breakers on the roof?"

I didn't know about any breakers. To me, a breaker is a big wave on the beach. If there were breakers on the roof, we must have been under a flood.

"I don't think so," I said. "Not that I remember."

I wasn't much further ahead when I phoned a TV shop and asked the proprietor about the puzzling case of my lonesome set.

"Do you have rabbit ears?" he asked. At least I understood this; I knew he wasn't making fun of me.

"Yes."

"Is there a roof antenna in the condo too?"

"Yes, I understand there is."

"Well then, you'll probably find they were both connected to your TV set. That overloaded it, which caused the flipping. When you walked up the TV, some of the signals went into you; then it wasn't overloaded any more and it stopped flipping."

"You mean I'm full of radio signals now?"

"In a way."

It gave me quite a lift: I never knew I had a magnetic personality. Any day now, walking along the sidewalk, I may suddenly hear my gold tooth playing "Can I Have This Dance for the Rest of My Life?"

Meanwhile, I've had lots of good advice. The most recent technician who came to fix the heating-air-conditioning system, Charlie Wolff, a really huge man, assured me it's simple to keep a TV performing at its best.

"I had a set that didn't flip over. Instead the whole picture kept falling down the right side," he said, "just as if the foundation had been dynamited.

"Well, I found out if I went up to that set and gave it a little pat on the top – not a slap, you understand – just a friendly pat, it came back okay right away.

"Some TV sets, you see, are in the habit of kicking up a fuss when all they need is a little lovin'."

I told myself that if Charlie, this six-foot-five giant weighing 290 pounds, could be that tender to his temperamental TV, the least I could do was try.

However, a lady a few houses down the lane informed me patting a TV was a lot of nonsense.

"I talk to my plants," she said, "and you've seen how wonderfully they grow.

"So I say, talk to your TV. Make it feel wanted! This can't do any harm, and you might be surprised."

So if you happen to be strolling past my window someday, and the TV weatherman is saying, "A severe cold front is approaching from Canada, and the temperature tonight may drop to 30°," you may hear me say, "Don't you worry your little picture tube, my pet; I'll adjust the heat for 72° all night. Daddy wouldn't want you to get a cold and start talking hoarse, would he? Sweet dreams, love!"

Well, whatever you think, talk's cheaper than hiring a TV repairman these days.

All the Better
To Eat You With

There is just one thing that disconcerts me more than
sitting in a homeward-bound bus across from a
woman trying to control a rebellious, squirming child.
It is to hear her whisper darkly, indicating me with her
head, "That man will get you if you don't sit still."

The boy, suddenly quiet, looks at me wide-eyed.

"He's a monster," she says in a low undertone, delighted by the effect I am achieving. As a matter of information she adds, "He eats little boys for supper."

This makes me uneasy. I frown uncomfortably,
which, I realize, only makes me look fiercer. I wish I
had shaved. I ask myself if she would say that about
any man, or if I look more monstrous than I thought.
Several passengers near her whisper to each other and
smile at me, but quickly glance away when I face them.

I clear my throat loudly to imply I can hear every
word; but she confides eagerly in his ear, "Better sit
still – he's growling at you."

In an effort to show the youngster I'm really good-
natured, I force myself to smile broadly at him. But I
can't smile artificially anyway, and it's worse when I
am frowning.

"He's looking mad at you," she whispers ominously.
"Do you see his sharp teeth?"

I shut my mouth quickly. A skinny woman beside me
gets up and moves across to a seat opposite. She may

want a different view of the countryside, or she may want to keep me in sight so I can't eat her by surprise, though she flatters herself if she thinks she would make one good meal.

In despair I try putting my hand to my forehead, partly covering my face, and study my coat buttons.

"He's thinking about you," the faint whisper says above the engine's hum. "Stop fidgeting. He may jump anytime now."

But she has overdone a good thing. A wail fills the bus: "I don't want the man to eat me up."

Passengers farther up the aisle mutter angrily. They have managed to get the idea I am threatening to devour the child and the mother is endeavouring to calm his fears.

I attempt to grin cheerily at the mutterers, but they don't change their expressions. They think I am inviting them to enjoy the fun, and their glares reflect that they don't appreciate my idea of a joke.

With relief I notice my bus stop is approaching, so I pull the cord and get up; but the bus slows suddenly and I lurch across the aisle. The boy shrieks. A woman's exasperated voice from the rear exclaims, "He *won't* stop tormenting that child," and another says, "He should be reported."

As I start to step off the bus, I see my wife hurrying to meet it. "Quick!" she shouts. "Go back and see if there's a woman with a little boy on board. She's Mrs. Johnson. I'm to look after her son while she goes on to the bridge at Mabel's."

"Well – what – what will I say?" I stammer, still standing on the step as the driver nudges me to get off.

"Just say to the boy," she pants, pushing me up the steps, "that you would like to have him for supper."

I gulp and seize her arm and lead her quickly towards the house as the bus roars off. "I didn't need to look," I say, "because there were no kids on the bus."

Technological Improvements I Would Like To See in the Interests of a Good Night's Nap

A dripless sink
  Without a tap

A felt-lined door
  Without a rap

A king-size blind
  Without a gap

A storm without
  A thunderclap

A bough that breaks
  Without a snap

But this may be too much to hope for:

A next-door spitz
  Without a yap

"You'll Just Roar
at Gert's Letter"

I t is very difficult to laugh when I am supposed to, especially if I am calling on the new neighbour up-stairs and he hands me a letter: "Here's something that will kill you. It's from our daughter Gert, out in Kansas City. You'll just *roar* at Gert."

His family gathers around and watches my face with expectant eagerness, waiting to see me just roar if not get killed outright.

Now, I have no doubt that Gert kept the household in fits of merriment before she moved away. But I have never even met her. Nevertheless I have to laugh at the letter or they will all wonder what is the matter with me. I have to laugh particularly loud because I am call-ing to persuade Gert's father to join the Caribou Fraternal Society, which needs new members and their fees badly. The fear of not being able to laugh to their satisfaction grips my heart and numbs my reactions.

I begin reading, or try to, in a tense atmosphere punctuated by the anticipatory giggles of Gert's sisters and muffled guffaws from her father as they wait for me to be killed. I can hardly concentrate on the words. Instead of reading, I keep wishing I were one of those follows who can turn belly laughs on and off as easily as a tap.

Frantically I scan down the lines, hoping to be seized by a paroxysm of mirth, but nothing happens. I might as well be reading the county fair prize list, the letter is

120

so dull. My spirits fall completely when I finally come to: "... keep smiling – yours as ever – Gert." I dare not look up, frozen-faced, so I pretend to be still engrossed in the letter and pray for the ceiling plaster to fall and distract everyone's fixed gaze.

Puzzlement clouds the faces in the parlour. "You must be a slow reader," muses Gert's mother. "You haven't come to the funny places yet."

"No," I manage to smile painfully, "I'm just getting into it."

Staring helplessly at "yours as ever – Gert," I hear her kid sister whisper, "He'll die when he comes to the place where she tells the bill collector to light his pipe with the money and he says he doesn't smoke."

Figuring that this excerpt, which I can't even remember reading, is a good thing to roar at, I burst out in the liveliest laugh I can simulate: "Ha, ha, ha! Say, this is wonderful! This bill collector's a scream! Oho, ho, ho, ho!"

Everyone's face brightens up immediately as they see I am a person of intelligence who really appreciates Gert.

Then Gert's father, who has been rummaging through his pockets for more of her letters to kill me with, says, "Hey, wait a minute. *Here's* the letter about the bill collector. You must have the one where the landlord puts Gert out on the street. That was the sad one. We all felt like crying."

Now they all look put out by my callousness to Gert. I realize there is no point in prolonging the situation. I am incapable of laughing naturally now, and they will recognize my artificial laugh if they hear it again.

So I flee down the stairs on the first excuse I can think of – that I'm sure I left the gas turned on.

Now they not only wonder what is the matter with me, but they expect me to blow up the house any day. Gert's father is not a member of the Caribou Fraternal Society, but neither have I got around to asking him. Why rush people into organizations, anyway, when you don't even know if they will make good members?

Fireman,
Save That Cup!

W ell, has our fire brigade ever been having fun competing for the J. W. F. Brownswatt, MP, District Trophy!

"My silver cup," Mr. Brownswatt said proudly, "is designed to stimulate friendly rivalry between the Millvale and Grasstown volunteer departments. Whichever arrives first at more fires this year will be the winner. And I trust that the property owners who benefit will remember their gratitude to me next election."

The MP's idea was sure a smart one. The friendly rivalry has increased like a house afire. A good illustration was the blaze last week in the old Barker dump, five miles from here.

Boy, was *that* a close one! Only by the merest stroke of good luck did we Millvale fellows escape a humiliating defeat.

It just happened that our deputy sub-chief, Dan Polker, sprinting down the highway to meet our fire truck, saw the Grasstown truck roaring up in the lead. Dan had the presence of mind to grab a pitchfork and pose as a farmer, directing them down the wrong road, or they'd have beaten us to it.

Due to the fact that our own truck broke down a moment later, a Grasstown undercover agent having put sand in the carburetor, we didn't get to the fire either.

But at least we'd earned a tie (one point); those Grasstown sneaks hadn't humbled us. In appreciation we unanimously elected good old Dan a full sub-chief. We heard later the dump burned up. The Barkers should have been more careful about it anyway.

Dan was the hero of another fire the very next day. When the Mercer sawdust pile started going up, our sub-chief acted in a flash. He phoned his cousin, near the mill, and offered the kids a quarter to stand out in the road and tell the Grasstown brigade the fire was already out.

This enabled us to pass them standing still – and you should have seen their faces when we doused them with high-velocity vapour spray! Unfortunately the next minute our front tires blew – I *knew* there was something suspicious about the "new county inspector" who visited our fire station the night before – but we Millvale boys aren't the kind to give in easily. We hoisted the truck across the road just in time to catch the Grasstown truck headlong. They won't soon forget the drenching they took from our hoses before they had a chance to regain their senses!

Altogether it was a wonderful day, and we elected Dan permanent chief. Oh yes – the sawdust pile. It burned up. It was no good anyway.

For some reason, the ratepayers of Millvale and Grasstown have since held an emergency meeting and decided to amalgamate the two brigades immediately. Mr. Brownswatt has announced he will offer his trophy instead for the prettiest garden in the county, and hopes the householders will remember their gratitude to him at an appropriate time.

Personally I think they're making a great mistake; they're taking away the healthy competitive spirit that's made our brigades what they are. Chief Dan Polker feels it's all a jealous move by Grasstown to prevent us from winning the cup.

"It would serve the property owners right," he says, "if we refused to put out any more of their old fires."

How We Made
Mr. McQuill's
Christmas Merrier

P lease tell me," said Inspector Hawkloft quietly, "any possible clues you can suggest concerning what happened to Sylvester J. McQuill."

Well (I told him), I don't imagine I can help you much, but here goes:

I always like to see people get enjoyment out of Christmas cards. That was one thing that stood out about Sylvester McQuill. He just *loved* Christmas cards! He'd start shopping for them in October, badgering Mr. Crumley the stationery store manager to get him something distinctive, something nobody else would be sending out.

"Yes," said Inspector Hawkloft, quietly making notes. "Please go on."

It was (I went on) two years ago that I first called at his boarding house on Christmas Eve. I shook hands with Mr. McQuill warmly and wished him a Merry Christmas.

But he shook his head. "You can't expect me to feel happy this Christmas," he said. "People don't like me."

He just brooded and wouldn't explain. But later his kindly old landlady, Mrs. Peabody, confided to me his bitter secret – he'd sent out eighty-nine cards and got back only seventy-three!

"Mr. McQuill refused to eat his supper," she said in great distress. "He just sat by the Christmas tree counting his cards over and over, trying to figure out who hadn't sent him any and why they should be mad at him. He's terribly angry with the postman for not bringing more, and simply furious with Mr. Crumley because two of the greetings he got were the same as he sent out – the 'Winter Hackmatack Forest' card."

Inspector Hawkloft broke in quietly, "I remember the occasion quite well. That was the Christmas Day Mr. McQuill phoned my house at six AM and demanded I investigate a postman who was suspected of keeping back some of his greeting cards. Please continue."

Well (I continued), on Christmas Eve the next year I took the precaution of phoning Mrs. Peabody before supper and asking her how the situation stood. The dear old soul was overjoyed! She could hardly wait for Mr. McQuill to arrive home and see all the cards – he'd got more this time than he sent out!

So I dropped in later and shook Mr. McQuill's hand warmly and wished him a Very Merry Christmas, because naturally I knew he'd feel enthusiastic about how popular he was.

But he shook his head glumly. "A lot of people are annoyed at me this Christmas," he said. "You see, I got 104 cards – but I only sent out ninety-two! What must the other twelve people be thinking of me?"

He fretted all evening. He was inconsolable. Poor Mrs. Peabody told me he was simply raging at the postman for bringing him so many cards. He was mad at Mr. Crumley too, for some reason.

Inspector Hawkloft observed quietly, "I remember the occasion quite well. That was the Christmas he woke me at five AM and insisted I arrest a Mr. Crumley for false pretences because he had received six cards of the same kind Mr. Crumley sold him as exclusive – 'Cherubs in a Snowfall,' I think it was. Kindly proceed."

Well (I proceeded), *this* Christmas I realized there was one thing I could do for the peace of mind of Mr. McQuill and his lovable old landlady: I could personally see that he got exactly as many cards as he sent out, no more and no less.

So I bought a dozen cards from Mr. Crumley – mak-

125

ing sure, of course, they were different from the "Pixies Throwing Snowballs" card which Mr. McQuill had bought. I signed them with vague names like "Jack" and "Dick" and "Fred" and addressed them all to Mr. McQuill.

As Christmas approached, I kept in touch with Mrs. Peabody and the postman. Whenever cards for Mr. McQuill were arriving too thick and fast, she hid a few in the bookcase. Whenever they began to slump, she brought out the hidden cards and added some of the special ones I had given the postman to deliver. The idea was that Mr. McQuill would finally have an even hundred cards – the same number he had mailed.

"Yes," said Inspector Hawkloft quietly, "the case is becoming quite clear now. Please resume your story."

Well (I resumed), on Christmas Eve, which was tonight, I called in and shook Mr. McQuill's hand warmly and wished him a Joyously Merry Christmas, because I knew this time he would be delighted.

But he shook his head in despair.

"It's not such a Merry Christmas as you think," he said. "My cards are driving me crazy!"

I asked him why.

"Because," he said, "I sent out a hundred cards and I got a hundred back – but some of the people I sent to didn't send to me, and some of the people who sent to me I didn't send to, and as they just signed their first names I can't figure out who they are so I can get Mr. Crumley to open up his store and sell me enough cards to send back to them tonight, that is if I can get the postman to come and pick up the cards so they can be date-stamped before midnight – and when I *do* see Crumley will I ever give *him* an earful, because I got *eight* 'Pixie Throwing Snowballs' –"

It was precisely at that moment (I said) when I drew out the revolver and shot him.

The *bang!* seemed strangely to echo more than once, which was explained when I noticed that dear sweet old Mrs. Peabody, across the room, also had a smoking revolver in her hand. Further, I may say, I perceived that the front window was shattered and a postman was walking down the street whistling merrily and tossing a revolver into an ash can. It was then, also, that Mr. Crumley stepped out beaming from behind the living-room drapes, pocketed a smoking revolver, and, remarking that he had just dropped in, apologized that he couldn't stay as he had to hurry home and prepare his house for "the Merriest Christmas yet."

It was not, you understand, Inspector, that any of us had anything against Mr. McQuill. It merely occurred to all of us that he would have a much happier Christmas if he didn't have the cards on his mind.

So as I said at the start, I don't think I can help you much. I really haven't the slightest idea who shot him. By the way, Inspector, how did you happen to reach the scene so quickly? It seemed no sooner did Mr. McQuill hit the floor a few moments ago than you climbed out of the hot-air vent.

"It was," Inspector Hawkloft said quietly, "pure coincidence." And, after jotting down in his notebook the words "committed by person or persons unknown," he quietly took a revolver from his pocket, blew through the chamber, sending a puff of blue smoke out the end of the barrel, replaced it in his pocket, said "A Merry Christmas to all" and strolled home with me for a cup of coffee and a sandwich.

The Remarkable Cure
of Horace Bivins

I like Horace Bivins, but I don't like his habit of coming up behind people, putting his hands over their eyes and chuckling, "Three guesses who."

Everybody knows who it is, and it is no fun for anybody except Horace. It makes me feel conspicuous when he catches me in a public place; passers-by get the impression they are seeing, in the post-office lobby, two grown men who have never quite got over the wonderful times they had in kindergarten.

The way to cure him, I realized, was to let him find out how *he* liked it.

So I crept up behind him the other evening in the Regal Hotel lobby, clamped my hands over his eyes, sending his glasses spinning into the palm stand, and exclaimed, "Three guesses who!"

Evidently it was a stunning surprise, but he took it good-naturedly. He kept walking slowly.

"Alderman Henderson?" he asked. My fingers could feel his face smiling.

"Guess again."

"Alderman Burkitt?" His voice sounded unnaturally deep. My fingers could also feel a moustache now; this was a little puzzling because I didn't remember Horace Bivins having a moustache.

"One more guess."

"Could it be – gracious, it must be – the mayor himself?" he asked excitedly. "It was not hard to guess, Your Worship; you see, I've met only you three gentlemen since I arrived in your city this afternoon."

The horrible fact dawned on me that I had only bothered to notice the familiar-looking topcoat and the back of the head. Who was this imposter?

"Oh, it isn't the mayor," I said, as buoyantly as I could. We kept walking helplessly, with the uncertain gait of two men inside a carnival horse.

"I give up," he repeated, waiting.

"No, no," I implored. "*You* wouldn't give up *that* easily." It was clear that he was a man whose inflexibility of determination I had long admired.

"I used up my three guesses," he insisted with a trace of annoyance. He stopped in his tracks, and I had to boost him sharply with my knee to overcome this show of obstinacy. It didn't matter where we were going, as long as we got out of the lobby. People were staring, and I tried to smile back cheerily in the hope we looked like two audience participants doing a stunt for a truth-and-consequences program.

"Make it *four* guesses," I urged as we stumbled into the corridor leading to the barbershop. I couldn't keep this up, I knew, but I couldn't let go of him either.

"I – I can't imagine," he stammered. "Are you from home in Wichita?"

"No," I answered, propelling him with my knee again because he had halted, though undoubtedly he thought it was a penalty for a poor guess.

We were coming to the entrance to the ladies' powder room. The door was ajar.

129

"This is extremely odd," he said, with his hands now crossed anxiously behind him. "We must have met at Cornell. There were some fellows in my –"

I didn't hear the rest. It was drowned in shrill feminine screams as I brought up my knee suddenly – he probably thought I didn't like Cornell – and heaved him headlong into the room. I slammed the door and fled out the side exit.

This effectively cured Horace Bivins. I understand that the visitor, whose name I never found out, made pointed inquiries around town, looked up Horace and gave him a terrific dusting-out. Horace has never since asked for three guesses. He is doomed to spend the remainder of his life trying to guess who.

I Meet Such
Interesting People

I don't know why I can't seem to be introduced to strangers properly when I go into a crowded living room. It's almost as if they try to catch me unawares; they always stand in the wrong places. I can't pick them out.

When my hostess excitedly says, "Oh, I want you to meet George Hackley!" and leads me into the room, exclaiming, "George, I'd like to present an old friend," I go straight to a stranger whose face has brightened up in a smile, grasp his hand and say, "Pleased to meet you, Mr. Hackley."

"*This* is George over here," the hostess says with a twinkle in her eye, standing beside another man. "That's Henry Biddle."

"Glad to meet you, too, Mr. Biddle," I hurriedly mumble, wheeling around. By the time I say "Mr. Biddle" I've got George Hackley's hand, and he says dryly, "I'm Hackley – that was Biddle you just shook hands with."

"I know, I know," I blurt, as if I always like to meet new friends when I'm turning around.

My hostess is rattling on, "And *Mrs.* Hackley" – with mock reproach – "you haven't even spoken to *Mrs.* Hackley."

I whirl about, striving to see where the hostess is looking, and I bow to an extraordinarily young woman who seems to be smiling. "How do you do, Mrs. Hackley!"

"Mrs. Hackley is over here," my hostess explains testily as everyone titters. "You're looking at her daughter Jane."

"Oh!" I do a quick turnaround and, in gathering confusion, say to the buxom dowager, "Pleased, I'm sure, Mrs. Jane."

"Mrs. *Hackley*" – my hostess' annoyed voice – "and behind you, Jane, her daughter."

I pivot again. "Glad to meet you, Miss Daughter."

"Miss *Hackley*. And now the Biddles – this is Mrs. Biddle."

I swerve, facing my hostess. "Pleased to biddle you."

"No, no – *behind* you" – her voice is rising.

"Pleased to behind you."

"No! Pleased to Mrs. Biddle behind you."

I whirl again helplessly. "Pleased to please you," I say, totally disconcerted, finding myself now bowing to my hostess.

"Delighted, I'm sure," she says and, seizing my hand, throws me over her shoulder into the hall.

"And So, Rise and Drink the Bride with Me"

The easiest task of all at a wedding is proposing the toast to the bride.

There seems to be a strange idea going around among men who are currently faced with this happy little chore, and who keep walking back and forth in their bathrooms muttering "Ladies and gentlemen" and addressing the full-length mirror on the door as if it was a lot of people, that it isn't easy at all. They say, in fact, it's the worst god-awful job they ever got into.

Isn't that silly? Why, there's nothing to it! I know; I did it.

I'll admit I had a few misgivings myself after I accepted the invitation. It seemed so easy to agree to at the time. "Certainly," I said, "I'd be delighted," and dismissed the thought. I vaguely imagined myself hoisting a glass, saying in a loud clear voice, "The bride!" and everyone nodding approval and murmuring, "The bride."

Not until several days afterward did it hit me with numbing impact that the toast called for a speech. The wedding was less than a fortnight away.

I hurried to Fred Frolley. He'd proposed the toast at a big wedding last year.

"It's simple," he told me buoyantly. "The caterer's wife is always there to signal you when to start. You just say some nice things about the girl, toss in a few jokes and end up with, 'And so now, ladies and gentlemen, it gives me great pleasure to propose the toast to the bride.' "

"Say – that doesn't sound bad at all!"

"Of course not. But you want to remember not to do – *ha, ha, ha!* – what Walter Holburn did! He was so fond of the bride – knew her since she was a little tot – he broke down right in the middle of it. Couldn't finish. Cried like a baby. But it's a cinch, really."

I thanked goodness the little tot in my case had been nineteen when I first met her.

Next day I bumped into Walter Holburn. I told him what I had to do. He didn't seem dismayed in the least, or even surprised.

"It's duck soup," he said ebulliently. "Nobody listens to you anyway. Of course, you don't want to do – *ha, ha, ha!* – what Fred Frolley did at the Ames girl's wedding reception. Boy oh boy" – Walter nearly doubled up laughing – "will I ever forget Fred!"

"What did he do?"

"*Ho, ho, ho!* What didn't he do! Fred got so jittery beforehand he even thought of taking a job up in the Yukon; if he wasn't in town, he couldn't be expected to give the toast. He went to the doctor, hoping he would be found sick and have to go to the hospital. As a last resort he took a four-week public-speaking course. Finally he primed himself with a flask behind every bush on the way to the reception, and there were a lot of bushes. When Fred got up to speak" – Walter

Holborn was holding onto me for support, he was laughing so hard – "he just smiled glassy-eyed and slowly sank to the floor! But, of course, we never told him. We all said, when he came to, it was a wonderful toast. But *you* won't have that trouble – you'll find it's a cinch."

Bill Bartley gave me similar assurance on his personal word, adding, however, "But don't make the mistake Herb Frobisher made – he rambled on endlessly for thirty minutes because he couldn't think of how to end it!"

And Herb Frobisher, when I asked him, beseeched me only to avoid the absent-minded error of Bill Bartley. "Bill had a matchbook with notes on it but got so flustered he couldn't find it, and stood there slapping frantically at his pants pocket, his coat pocket, his hip pocket, his watch pocket, until everybody in the room started scratching, thinking the place was full of fleas. But *you'll* see it's as easy as falling off a log. That is, unless it's one of those wet receptions."

"Are they bad?"

"Terrible! Everybody's hilarious. Nobody listens. And those who do always heckle you."

"Thank heaven," I said with relief. "This one's dry."

"Gosh, that's tough! They'll all freeze up on you. But don't worry – *you'll* make out all right."

Fortified by such positive reassurances on all sides, it was only natural I was full of confidence the week before the wedding.

I was so full if it, in fact, it gave me indigestion. I kept waking up with a start in the middle of the night, thinking I was being chased by head-hunters on the Amazon. When it dawned on me that I was home in bed, and was confronted by nothing more formidable than a toast to a bride, I felt worse. As I couldn't go back to sleep, I decided to rehearse my speech in my mind just for one last time.

My wife's voice suddenly crackled in the dark:

"Who are you talking to?"

135

"Me? Nobody," I said, surprised. "*I'm* not talking."

"I could have sworn you said, 'It's a great pleasure.' "

"Not *me*." This sounded as if the bed was full of people; but I was sure I hadn't been talking.

She didn't forgive me for several days. It wasn't that I woke her up; it was all the compliments she insisted I was paying to some girl in my sleep – "charming," "beautiful," and asking everybody to admire her youthful gracefulness.

I didn't explain to her. She'd only get the wrong idea. She'd think my speech was worrying me.

It wasn't, of course. I had gone over it so many times in my mind to get it letter-perfect, after spending three long evenings writing it out, how could it worry me? Just to be doubly sure, I kept repeating it every day as I worked, as I walked through the office, as I ate lunch, as I window-shopped, as I rode home on the bus.

My fellow passengers didn't help much.

A middle-aged man sitting beside me said, out of a blue sky, "It gives me great pleasure too."

"What does?"

"The scenery. Isn't that what you meant? Didn't you say it gave you great pleasure?"

"I didn't say a word."

I hadn't, as far as I knew. That's just how nosey some people are. He was trying to trick me into telling him about my speech.

If I hadn't been so full of confidence, I don't think I could ever have got through the wedding day. There was, for instance, the awful discovery I made early in the morning. (It happened to be four AM, and for some reason I didn't feel like sleeping and I was pacing the kitchen in my pyjamas, reciting my speech over for the very last time.) I found to my horror that I had learned the words so well that now they didn't mean anything to me. I was saying, "The bride is a lovely wedding, and I ask you all to drink her." After I put my head under the tap, the words came out fine again.

And there was that panicky feeling during the church

ceremony. The hushed atmosphere weighed down so heavily on me, sitting there in the front pew with the sunlight slanting softly through the stained-glass windows, and the voice of Rev. Mr. Hoskwith echoing so piously, and everybody so religious, and the saints solemnly looking down and contemplating me, I realized my intended speech was too flippant – it was entirely out of keeping with this holy occasion. I had to change it! I pondered furiously.

"For Pete's sake," my wife whispered in my ear, "stop mumbling; everyone's staring at you!"

"I'm not saying a word," I whispered back irritably.

"Then *don't*. Let Mr. Hoskwith run the service!"

I saw it was too late to change my speech. I tried to, but I couldn't – not with my wife continually nudging me, kicking my ankle, and elbowing me.

She was obsessed with the idea I was talking out loud. Even the clergyman had the same impression – he may have got it from watching her – because I saw him smiling and nodding at me; he thought I was repeating the prayers after him.

Then came the mad excited swirl of cars from the church to the reception. If the Rev. Hoskwith could have seen me in our car he would have been happy beyond belief, because I was still sitting with head bowed, muttering, as my wife drove on.

But I was really brimful of confidence. While it may be true that I couldn't seem to grab hold of the bride's hand to shake it in the reception line – I kept snatching for it and missing it – this wasn't because my hand was trembling with nervousness, as my wife thought, but because the bride's was. And as for my wife telling everyone afterward that I congratulated the groom by exclaiming vacantly, "Many *of* them!" as he captured my hand and shook it, I'm sure she misunderstood my words. I don't remember exactly what I said, due to the fact I was going over my speech in my head for the absolute last time, but I'm certain it was something appropriate.

Then amid the noisy hubbub of the sea of conversation I saw a smiling woman in the crowd fixing me with a gleaming eye and nodding her head agitatedly at me – I kept nodding back, wondering where I'd met her and trying to twist my face up into a smile – and my wife said, "That's the signal, you fool – *start*!"

Convulsively I clutched the tiny card in my pocket on which I had written the key lines of my toast, in letters so small I couldn't possibly have read them anyway even if my hand had been steady: "It's not only a great honour. . . . But to her parents' credit I must say. . . . As you know, she has always. . . . Which reminds me of the Italian serenader who. . . . So, you can see, she truly. . . . And so, ladies and gentlemen, it gives me. . . ."

Then an amazing thing happened.

"LADIES AND GENTLEMEN," said a loud strange voice. A sudden chorusing of "*Shhhhh-hh-hh-hh*!" sizzled around the room as if steam was escaping everywhere. "It is not only a great honour but also a happy privilege –"

Someone was giving my speech!

I saw everyone looking at me, the ladies with their heads cocked to one side, smiling the way they do at a budgie taking a bath. I realized to my surprise that it was me speaking.

I didn't have to do a thing.

I just listened.

The voice from nowhere rang out strong and loud, wondrously self-possessed except for what I recognized as an agonized undertone in every syllable.

I marvelled at how the voice rattled off the lines without missing a single cue – although in the sixty or seventy times I had rehearsed the speech I always muffed it somewhere and interjected "Oh, *cripes*!" and started again with new hopefulness, "Ladies and gentlemen –"

Then all eyes abruptly switched from me to the groom, and I knew I must have finished.

Gratefully I fished the little card out of my pocket to

see whether I could have read my notes if I had to. Just knowing it was there had bolstered me. I gasped. It said, in neat type:

Johnson's 8-Hour Dry Cleaning
"Back To You Before Day Is Thru"
16 Regent Street   Phone 9-9999

My own card was in my other suit! I braced myself against the mantel, as I suddenly felt faint. I think it was the heat.

Early the next week I ran into Fred Frolley and Walter Holburn on the street.

"Well!" said Fred cheerily. "Still alive! I'll bet you found the toast was no trouble at all."

"Not a bit," I said, still dazed. "It was a cinch." This was true. I wasn't even conscious of giving it.

"A fellow just needs confidence," Walter affirmed. "Of course, ha, ha, there's always that terrible moment during the church service when you think your very informal speech won't possibly do –"

"Did *you* feel that too?"

"Certainly. Everyone does. I changed mine, then changed it back again when I saw how slap-happy everybody was at the reception."

"And it *does* knock you out for a week or so before the wedding," Fred Frolley recollected.

"And three days after," Walter added.

"That's right," Fred amended approvingly. "A week before and three days after. But apart from that it's easy."

"Yes," agreed Walter. "Any fool can do it."

Oddly enough, neither Fred nor Walter to my knowledge, nor Bill nor Herb, has proposed the toast to the bride a second time. Neither have I, nor do I intend to. We'd be pretty poor sports if we didn't give other fellows a chance to see how easy it is.

139

Crop Forecast:
Bigger and Better

Minutes of Conference of Department Managers of Modern Perfection Seed Company in Office of General Manager, Mr. Bristlebloom, March 23, at three PM:

M r. Bristlebloom (briskly): "Well, you know why we're here – sales of our Himalaya Mammoth Pumpkin seeds have fallen off 30 per cent! I want to know *why*. Were our customers displeased with Himalaya Mammoth last year?"

Mr. O'Flaherty, Consumer Research: "No, sir – delighted! Our statistics show eighty-six old customers out of a hundred are reordering. But there are practially no *new* customers."

Mr. Bristlebloom: "Good heavens! Could Himalaya Mammoth have been left out of the spring catalogue?"

Mr. Schlatz, Catalogue Production: "No, sir! Here it is – see? – on page forty-eight – 'Himalaya Mammoth, Superlatively Prolific and Rapid Growing, Peerless Monarch of the Pumpkin World, Vegetable Pride of the Atomic Age –' "

Mr. Bristlebloom: "Well, not bad, but obviously worded a little too modestly. That's probably – HOLY SMOKE! Look at the *illustration*! Schlatz, did you approve this abomination? There's your trouble! The pumpkin looks to weigh no more than forty pounds! And *one* man is carrying it! Why, I've *seen* pumpkins that big!"

Mr. Schlatz (humbly): "Sorry, sir. A new young artist

made the sketch from an actual snapshot. He thought –"

Mr. Bristlebloom: "He *thought*! Does he think any amateur gardener in his right senses will buy seeds for a pumpkin that one man can carry? When the Ace-High Seed House has two men struggling to lift their Gorgeous Sonic-Speed-Growing Goliath?"

Mr. Schlatz: "He was trying –"

Mr. Bristlebloom: "He was only trying to belittle the Himalaya Mammoth, that's what! A forty-pounder indeed! Does he want gardeners to think a Himalaya Mammoth is a midget? You know as well as I do it can hit twenty pounds! This is malicious misrepresentation; the fellow is probably in the pay of Ace-High Seed House. Check his security file."

Mr. Schlatz: "Perhaps if we put out our second run of catalogues with *three* men struggling to lift a Himalaya Mammoth –"

Mr. Bristlebloom (happily): "Right on! That's the spirit! Now you're talking! Three men – one of them with a look of anguish on his face to show he's pulled a groin ligament! Get it? And let's make it a record-breaking 200-pound pumpkin while we're at it! Have we ever grown anything that big in the catalogue?"

Mr. Schlatz (thoughtfully): "Well, we grew a Glory of the Universe Hybrid White Spine Cucumber right across a two-page spread in 1949; it must have weighed forty-five pounds –"

Mr. Bristlebloom: "Come, come! Surely we've done better than that in good growing years."

Mr. Schlatz (slowly): "Yes, by jiminy, I do recall the art department cultivating an eighty-pound Royal Rajah Cabbage in '41 – the one that was breaking the back of the farmer in the picture –"

Mr. Bristlebloom: "Ah, yes – *there* was a beautiful illustration! Now, Schlatz, if we did that in '41 we can grow a whopping big pumpkin today.

"Let's show it being winched into a half-ton truck. Hell, never mind if it will really grow that big. Think of what keeps free enterprise growing. Think of it as Progress!"

But Where's
the Love Interest?

Scene: Boardroom of American Consolidated Pictures, Hollywood, California, following take-over by Happy Treat Soft Beverage Corporation. Presiding is Sol Rademaker, TV planning chief, who speaks:

Gentlemen, it gives me great pleasure to introduce Mr. John L. O'Harrity, the production genius of Happy Treat who will become our new president and board chairman. (Applause) Happily, sir, we can show you today a few rushes from our new pilot film, 'The Krazy Kids.' It looks like we've got a real bang-in-the-belly series if we just get it into the right time slot – should run for years."

Mr. O'Harrity: "Is it a show about children?"

"Hell, no. These three fellas in their teens are wild about fast cars, see? They're always racing around, but the police cars can never catch them."

"Why not?"

"Well, sir, with all due deference may I point out it would end the series if the three fun-loving boys were sentenced to jail by a long-nosed judge without any humour in him. Now, the rushes, please. . . . Hey, just lookit that! Did you ever see a more spectacular roll-over by a police car that got only its left wheels on the ramp? Whaddya think, boss?"

"Is that the big climax of the show?"

"Cripes, no! We smash up eleven police cars after they sail over that ramp – one goes into the drink, six burst into flames, four explode. During the chases we incidentally wipe out three police motorcycles, one plane, one helicopter, and two mock-up hangars."

"But isn't this wholesale demolition of vehicles pretty expensive?"

"It sure isn't peanuts, boss! However, you'll agree we've got to keep up with similar series on rival networks."

"But where's the love interest? I may be a little old-fashioned, but I thought every movie had a love interest."

"Well, you'll understand, of course, that by putting in a love sequence we'd have to eliminate at least four car smash-ups."

"Couldn't you put in just a little?"

"Come to think of it, a girl does come up behind one of the boys in a restaurant and put her arms around him – he doesn't pay any attention to her, of course – and she says, 'I want you.' It's just a little touch of romance, you will understand."

"Frankly, I don't understand. It never happened to me."

"Well, boss, how about this? You've seen all these

news stories about North American automobile production picking up? We're doing our share. We're buying more cars every week. It's a sort of patriotism."

"What about the stunt drivers? Don't they ever get injured?"

"Don't give them a thought. They're covered by insurance if they get a concussion or a broken leg or anything. It costs us a pretty penny to treat them so well."

"You'll forgive me, Mr. Rademaker, if I don't seem to grasp the reality of the situation. Shouldn't the Krazy Kids be put behind bars for destroying so many police vehicles and risking injury to the officers?"

"That's just it, boss. They never bump police cars off the road; the police come to grief themselves! It's their own fault. They're over-eager. The boys just laugh a lot – you know, full of high-spirited fun and jokes. They're good boys who don't hang around pool halls, they're real models to the upcoming generation."

In Every Home
It's a Merrie,
Merrie Yuletide

A British psychologist, Professor Hilland, says people shouldn't let themselves feel "down" just because they get into marital spats on Christmas Day.

"The trouble is," he asserts, "they build up an idealistic anticipation of 100 per cent joy reigning in every household. Then they feel somehow cheated when little disappointments crop up in their own. They should remember that every home has a balky stovepipe, a toothache, a burnt turkey in the oven, or a loud husband-and-wife argument at dinner."

I can't imagine where the professor got such strange ideas. I haven't heard of any burnt turkeys in my friends' homes at Christmas, nor any marital spats either.

Look at Herb Frobisher's house. Last Christmas there certainly wasn't any "loud husband-and-wife argument" there!

Herb, as a matter of fact, slept right through till noon, even with the kids banging drums. And I know there wasn't any chance of an argument the rest of the day, either, because Stella Frobisher wasn't speaking to him.

It had something to do with a Christmas Eve office party, and Herb rolling in at two AM just in time to insist he would finish the tree by going up the stepladder and putting the star on top. He finished it, too; he fell into it. It was fortunate that Stella had built such a strong plank base on the tree and braced it so well, because by hugging it tightly Herb just sank to the floor. Mrs. Frobisher got the tree up again by three AM, but didn't bother about Herb.

Which is not to say, of course, that all husbands are as neglectful of their duty of trimming the tree.

Bill Bartley came home bright and cheerful from the same noon-hour party quite early – it wasn't later than 10:45 PM – to find a note on the hall table:

"I've taken the phone off the hook and gone to bed. A lot of screaming women kept asking John (isn't it remarkable how much his voice sounds like yours now?) if this is where Elvis Bartley lives. Also, someone by name of Chickie wants to know why she didn't get a pair of nylons too. You'll find the ornaments in the closet."

Well, you never saw a husband so dutiful as Bill about putting real effort into decorating a tree all through the night. I'll say one thing for him, however: even though after wrapping the presents and all, he threw himself into bed just as the youngest shrilled "Santy was here!" and dragged him out again by one leg, he didn't say a cross word to Edna Bartley all day.

And what do you think Edna found when she opened the dressing gown he'd bought her? A twenty-dollar bill sticking out of the pocket! That's the kind of happy gesture husbands in this country dream up just on the spur of the moment.

Talk about Christmas marital joy. I heard that even Walter Holburn, who's always so crochety about his in-laws, rushed out to the bus stop to greet his mother-in-law Christmas morning and shouted, "Welcome home, Mother!"

That happened to be just after Jean Holburn picked up the shirt he'd worn the day before and said, in a strange voice, "That's not *my* lipstick."

Well, as I said, you never saw anyone so happy as Walter to see his wife's relatives and show them he was a good fellow. He loved them! In fact, he didn't want to see them leave again. He would have driven them all the way back to Plainville that evening in his own car – even though it meant he would have to be away from home on Christmas night – if Jean hadn't stopped him.

And Christmas dinner was a wonderfully joyous occasion! If any of those present were under the impression that Walter violently objected to eating by candlelight, something Jean always insisted on, they could see they were mistaken. In fact, Walter was the very first one to suggest it.

Possibly some had got that idea last year when Walter stuck his knife into the ball of yellow yarn beside his mother-in-law's plate, thinking it was the butter. This time, of course, he didn't do that; he was too smart. Besides, Jean had warned her mother not to bring her knitting to the table. When he *did* try to bite into a wax apple from the fruit centrepiece after the dessert, no one joined in the general merriment more heartily than Walter.

Just in case the cheeriness of my friends may seem to have some connection with Christmas Eve parties, I'd like to point to Sam McCool's home. There was a real illustration of marital harmony for you!

Sam, a fine-living man, didn't go out at all on Christmas Eve. When I asked him a few days later how Christmas went at his house, he said, "Oh, it was very congenial."

Were any angry words exchanged between husband and wife?

"No, not one," he said definitely.

That should show the British professor something!

It was, in fact, his best Christmas yet, Sam told me. The day began with a wonderful feeling of joy and relief when he woke up at eight AM and realized that the pup, which they'd smuggled into the house after midnight to surprise the kids, had kept quiet downstairs all night.

"I lay in bed congratulating myself," said Sam. "Of course, when I got downstairs I found the pup had eaten all the canes and popcorn off the tree, but was I ever lucky! He'd finished only six of the chocolates from the five-pound box, tinsel and all. I pretended Santa ate them. And I was able to wrap up the wife's slip again, after getting it out from under the stove with the broom. She never even guessed it had come in a box."

"But the rest of Christmas Day?" I persevered. "It was all a merry occasion?"

"Oh, yes, perfect! My cousin's family brought their kids in to see the tree, and was I lucky again – they carved up the old piano bench some with my new hunting knife, but not one of them thought of the new piano! And the wife's aunt dropped in unexpectedly just before Christmas dinner. You know her, she's the one who keeps clacking her teeth – and her uncle Frank, who keeps lighting up old stogies with his face right in the tree branches –"

"But you *did* enjoy Christmas dinner?"

"Absolutely. I sure did!"

That's pretty good proof of how happy an average family Christmas is in Canada.

Of course, Sam added, he didn't happen to be home for Christmas dinner himself. You see, he's a plumbing contractor, so naturally when the unexpected phone call came that the high-school water pipe had burst, Sam had no choice but to rush out of the house, putting on his hat and coat even though it meant leaving Aunt Carrie clacking her teeth on a barley toy right in the middle of her interesting story about how her other niece out in Saskatchewan had married so well.

As luck would have it, too, the water pipe proved so stubborn that Sam didn't get home until quite a while after supper – until the absence of cars at his door showed all the guests had gone.

"I had wieners and beans at Joe's Roadside Lunch near the school," he informed me. "That was my

148

Christmas dinner!" The way he said it, with such a brave smile, you could only admire him for staying so cheerful while he was missing all the treats at home.

He added, "My Christmas dinner cost me only $2.75 – seventy-five cents for Joe's and two dollars for the phone call."

I couldn't understand this – Sam hadn't mentioned making any phone call; besides, I think he must have been mistaken; phone calls are only twenty-five cents.

Anyway, the British professor certainly can't be speaking about Christmas conditions in Canada. As I said, I haven't heard of any loud husband-and-wife arguments in my friend's houses. And not one of them had a burnt turkey, either.

"Hello! Could I Give You Fifteen Silver Dollars?"

The good-looking young man was smiling so person-ably as he approached us on the Gulf of Mexico beach, not far from our winter home in Largo, Florida, I was sure we must have met him before.

"Would you like to be our guests at a wine-and-cheese party? We'd like very much to have you come."

I was flattered. I didn't know I was so popular.

"Who's having the party?"

"Our new time-sharing condominium at St. Peters-burg Beach. We just want you to see it! Everyone who inspects the beautiful apartments will receive five silver dollars – and a surprise gift."

You can't beat that for friendliness.

Only a few minutes later an attractive young blonde came along with a clipboard, pad and pen, and raised the bid.

"Hello! We'd love to have you come to our wienie roast tonight," she said, flashing an engaging smile.

"Who's giving the wienie roast?"

"Our new shared-time-interval condominium, right on the beach at Madeira. Oh, it's lovely! We're anxious to have you see it. And the best part is, after the tour every couple will be presented with fifteen silver dollars."

I had never seen such generosity!

We were too busy that evening to go from condominium to condominium gathering in all the gifts, but I soon discovered that many of my New Brunswick friends were being showered with silver too. Some opportunists were taking up all the offers, even though they came back a little shaken by their first experiences with high-pressure super-salesmanship.

One couple, who didn't have any intention of ever buying an apartment, went along anyway and made their supper out of hors d'oeuvres, cheese and wine, got their five dollars and the surprise gift – a lady's umbrella.

Isn't that wonderful?

Of course, there are skeptics who will tell you that the condominium builders, who are so compulsively addicted to raising new skyscrapers they can't shake the habit, aren't really philanthropists at all, but are desperate to find buyers. They're pushing the idea of "shared-time" apartments, which means twenty-six people each buy a two-week time interval in one apartment.

Through an exchange system they can take their two weeks there or in another time-sharing condominium, or, if they wish, another part of the country or another part of the world. An advantage to the developer is that it's easier to sell two weeks' worth than an entire fifty-two-week ownership, so he can collect a whopping aggregate price.

At least that's what the kill-joys tell you.

I prefer to believe the current outburst of money being tossed around is pure Florida hospitality to us "snowbirds" from the North.

I've now had several promises of fifteen silver dollars and, during a visit to the elite boutiques of St. Armand's Circle while driving down Sarasota way, an even better offer.

While I was talking with a younger New Brunswick tourist beside the curbside stone benches, where fearful husbands wait interminably for their wives to come out of the expensive shops, a handsome smiling youth

151

walked up to us and said, "Hi! Would you like to come to our cocktail reception at Lido Beach this evening? It will be a real party, and we're setting up volleyball nets on the beach for the younger guests."

This seemed an enticing offer, especially as he happened to add as an afterthought that many young women at Lido Beach were now going topless. But just then my wife came out of the boutique.

"We'll be gone by then," I told him firmly. "We're just here for the day."

"Well, okay!" he exclaimed happily. "It's now eleven AM. Tell you what: If you see our time-interval condominium by one PM you'll be given a certificate for this value."

He took out a fancy slip of paper that said we'd be entitled to merchandise worth twenty dollars. Then he crossed out the "twenty dollars" and wrote in "forty dollars" and initialled it.

Such munificence, I thought, only befitted an area where I noticed a sports shirt in a men's boutique bore a forty-seven-dollar price tag, and a rather nondescript windbreaker went for seventy-five dollars.

We didn't go but, human nature being what it is, I discovered that perhaps I was getting spoiled.

When anyone after that offered me only five silver dollars, I just looked disdainfully at him and kept going.

A St. Stephen couple whom I know accepted an offer to "visit our new condominium at Clearwater Beach and be our guests for dinner."

They were given a ten-dollar certificate for two dinners at Adam's Rib, where they had a delicious meal.

True, up to six PM dinner at Adam's Rib is only $4.95.

But I couldn't help thinking afterward it was kind of cheap of that condominium not to include the tip.

C'mon–You Can Forget Your Diet for Just One Day!

I t's hard to diet at any time of year.
Invariably I have found, when I begin a reducing routine at home, friends will immediately invite us for dinner and serve the hostess' pride and joy for dessert – her own famous deep lemon pie with meringue. She will beam happily at me to see how I like it, and feel put out if I don't ask for a second helping.

I always seem to start a diet just before the harvest season I've been looking forward to – fresh maple cream and maple syrup on buttered pancakes, or strawberries with sugar and cream, or new peas with fried salmon steaks, or buttered corn on the cob.

But the worst is the Christmas-New Year's holiday season.

I had lost eighteen pounds in a month, on doctor's orders, and was determined to lose twenty-five more, even though we were continuing to accept invitations to parties at friends' homes. This was a great mistake.

In the festive season you can't win.

At every holiday party the decibel level keeps rising until the din of high-pitched chatter nearly deafens my ears. Glasses tinkle, women giggle and scream at increasingly risqué jokes told by the men. Faces look flushed.

And at every party I hear the same refrain from the hostess.

"C'mon, c'mon! Surely you can forget your diet for just one day – it's New Year's Eve! What'll you have?"

"Oh, nothing, thanks. Perhaps just some soda water."

"Soda water?" She looks shocked.

Suddenly one of the hostess' women friends descends on us.

"What's the matter with him?" – looking down perplexed at me sitting there with a glum face.

"He won't eat or drink anything."

"Why not?"

"I don't know. I think he just likes to be ugly."

I try to manage a wan smile, as though the hostess had said a good joke. But nobody smiles back.

Next day – New Year's Day – the harassment continues. Every host and hostess thinks I should throw self-discipline to the winds. Everyone is under the impression it's the only invitation out I've received in the holiday season, so why not go hog-wild for once?

Just like the previous evening, I have to sit there awkwardly declining trays of fudge cookies and rum fruitcake with thick almond-paste icing which the hostess keeps pressing on me.

"No?" she says, obviously a trifle miffed.

"Thanks, but I'm trying to go easy."

"Don't you like my cooking?" – frowning.

"Oh, yes, you're a wonderful cook, as I always tell people, but –"

"Just a second!" She returns still frowning but trying to smile at the same time. Now she's carrying a tray of shortcakes with almonds in the middle.

"Here!" she says cheerfully. "These wouldn't hurt a baby."

"Thanks, but could I have a couple of soda crackers? No butter."

Again she looks hurt. Without a word she marches out into the kitchen, marches back with a plate with four soda biscuits on it, and strides away in a huff.

Later the sky really falls in – after I've tried my best to oblige by eating four toasted sardine rolls and figuring I've had all my calories for the entire day.

One of the laughing women guests comes two-stepping over to me and says, "I'm looking for your wife. I want to tell her we're all going on to Antonio's for his special Pizza Milan dinner!"

Desperately I try to locate my wife first to head off the idea, because I've been through this before.

In the restaurant, I know, merriment will reign unbounded. Everybody will have cocktails, while I sit there staring at my ice water.

When the waiter with the ankle-length white apron comes around to take my order, he bows and recites suavely, "Your pizza, *signor* – what combination will be your pleasure? With pepperoni, with bacon, with mushrooms, with olives?"

"Could I have a boiled egg?" – keeping my voice low.

The waiter looks down at me with undisguised scorn.

All conversation at the long table suddenly seems to have ceased. Everyone has eyes fixed on me.

"What's the matter with him, anyway?" I hear a lady guest's voice whisper. "Why is he such a spoilsport?"

"I don't know," says the erstwhile cocktail-party hostess. "Just likes to be ornery, I guess."

Her whispering friend replies, "I feel sorry for his wife."

Desire Under
the Mahoganies

"M ore people every year are discovering there is no
pastime so delightfully stimulating as collecting
antiques," says a trade journal.

I believe it. It's true. Just look at my maiden great-
aunt Phoebe. She got delightfully stimulated when she
began collecting antiques. She got practically delirious. When I met her outside a big department store
her eyes were agog with excitement. She was giggling
like a schoolgirl.

"Oh, *do* come in with me!" she pleaded. "There's a
perfectly darling chair in their antique department, but
I don't dare go in alone to look at it. The sales manager
has an *awful* crush on me. He talks so bold it makes me
all a-tingle, and I have to escape!"

I stared incredulously. "Good heavens! Did he actually –"

"Oh, no," she exclaimed, a little regretfully. "He
hasn't done anything *yet*; but, of course, I haven't given
him a fair chance. I've run away twice." She tittered.
"There's something unrestrained about him – a wild
Spanish streak or gaucho blood. Something exotic. *You*
know."

I nodded, to show I met men with wild Spanish
streaks and gaucho blood every day.

We went in. I prepared myself for anything.

But the middle-aged salesman with the four-in-hand

necktie looked harmlessly impersonal. When he saw Aunt Phoebe beaming at him, his face fell.

"Oh, yes," he began coldly, "the chair. Here it is, madam. Now as I was saying yesterday when you suddenly remembered your dental appointment, in this elegant old chair you have many fine features. You have, may I say, madam, a lovely curving back – and so gently scalloped. You have one of the most beautiful backs I have ever seen."

Aunt Phoebe coloured slightly and fluttered her eyelids.

"And," he went on, "your colouring is really superb – soft, lustrous, I suppose one might say honey blonde. Positively intriguing!"

He was gazing lovingly at the chair. Aunt Phoebe, blushing coquettishly, was scuffing the floor with her toe.

"Your arms," he said caressingly, "are divine – so graceful and shapely – classic and refined in the eighteenth-century tradition – very old, of course, but all the more desirable and precious because of it. They mutely invite the weary to seek solace."

Aunt Phoebe was nervously tugging at my elbow. I could sense she was getting panicky and wanted to escape again.

"And your legs!" he exulted. "Ah, but they are priceless! So exquisitely turned and beautifully tapered –"

Aunt Phoebe was swaying. She wheeled unsteadily to flee.

"– right down to your antique brass claw feet," continued the sales manager enthusiastically, although his face now reflected puzzlement.

Aunt Phoebe didn't hear. She was hurrying me to the doorway, whispering hoarsely, "Get me out of here. He's violent!"

Bewilderedly the sales manager called after her, "And I'm almost certain you have a solid walnut top – you're richly upholstered with fine quality horsehair – your joints may creak a little, but don't let that deceive you, for your sturdy frame will never warp because it's glue-blocked for rigidity –"

Aunt Phoebe was sprinting unheeding down the steps to the street, urging me to more speed. The sales manager shouted in desperation from the doorway, "Your back is washable, too. Just wipe with a damp cloth –"

His words faded into nothingness behind us.

"My soul!" gasped Aunt Phoebe at a safe distance. "Just think – if you hadn't saved me I'd have been in his clutches!"

She added with determination, "He won't get *me* – not today!"

I learned that Aunt Phoebe went back the very next day but found that her sales manager had been transferred to the chemical garden fertilizer department. He pretended to be polite, as always, but the remarks he made about me when showing off a package of garden conditioner were positively insulting.

"That's what unrequited love does," Aunt Phoebe said with a sigh. "They always turn nasty."

And she duly wrote him into her diary as another suitor she had turned down.

You Can't
Depend on Kids

W hen my children want to know something, they always come to good old Pop. He has the answers.

Like the day my younger boy, who's seven, asked me why a British expedition was planned to climb Mount Everest, because he had to say a piece about it at school.

"Just to get to the top," I said, smiling at the beautiful simplicity of my answer. Any child could understand it. That's the way to talk to children.

"Why," he asked, "do they want to get to the top?"

This was harder, but I was equal to it.

"For the very same reason that you fellows were trying yesterday to climb to the top of the spruce tree. Why was that?"

"Oh, I see now," he said happily. "There's a bird's nest up there."

"No, *no!*" I replied. "There isn't any bird's nest up there."

"How do you know," he asked seriously, "if nobody's been up there lately to see?"

"Well, I'm not absolutely sure, as far as that goes; but that's not why they're climbing the mountain."

"Then why are they?"

"Er – well, for the sense of achievement! Yes, that's it. For example, why did you feel so good about winning Skinny Glasby's marbles today?"

"Because he swiped my baseball mitt yesterday."

"He *did*? Not the good one I brought you from Boston?"

"Yep. He hid it, too, but I found it."

"That's the spirit! Now run and get it and we'll just have time for a little pitching warm-up before supper."

When my wife and I went to the parent-teacher meeting next night, I got a shock when the principal announced that my boy would read an essay on the Mount Everest expedition.

For an awful moment I thought he would say they were climbing the mountain to see if there were any bird's nests up there. Worse, he might even say his father told him!

But my fears proved groundless.

"The reason they are climbing the mountain," he concluded the speech, "is because Skinny Glasby hid their baseball mitts up there."

It brought down the house. Everyone laughed and clapped. The principal, who had started to frown, suddenly beamed. He remarked that the ending showed a lively imagination which should be encouraged, although, of course, the child had overlooked the obvious point that the British would more likely be cricket players.

I still don't see why the ungrateful little tyke couldn't have slipped in a mention somewhere about his father.

Why Do
Bathroom Scales
Act That Way?

Anyone who has tried to stick to a reducing diet knows about the baffling behaviour of bathroom scales.

You stand on them when you get up, feeling bad to think that after you eat you'll weigh at least a pound more.

But when you return from the breakfast table, you're surprised to discover you're a pound lighter.

Or, facing an appointment next day with the doctor (who will immediately test your progess by weighing you), you may skimp on meals – and find at suppertime you've gained two pounds.

My wife insists that our bathroom scales don't have an intelligence of their own, that they're not mocking me as I believe.

"They just read differently at different places on the floor," she explains, "and you keep unconsciously moving them around with your foot until you get the best reading.

"But sometimes you can't find the right spot – so you get a higher reading, even when you stand crooked or put all your weight on your right foot to try to bring down the needle."

"I never do that."

"You do. I watched you."

Of course, she is wrong.

If scales don't act peculiarly, why is it that when you get to the doctor's office, wearing your lightest suit, and kick off your shoes to help keep the reading down, and hope the doctor won't notice you're slipping your pocketbook and wristwatch into your coat pocket before taking off the coat itself – why is it that his big scales always register five pounds more than yours at home?

I know one man who in desperation even shoves his false teeth and his eyeglasses into the pocket, but it doesn't do any good.

My friend would gladly even stuff his toupee in too, but the doctor would be sure to notice the difference. He'd look around and say in puzzlement, "Where is that patient I had just before you came in?"

Isn't this a mischievous intelligence on the part of the scales? It must be. I'd hate to think the doctors themselves would be low enough to set the mechanism high so they could always diagnose with a sigh, "Well, we simply must start doing something about our weight." (That's what doctors always say even when they're thin as a rake. It's supposed to make you feel better.)

These thoughts came to mind the other day when I talked with a Sussex housewife who unquestionably has the most diabolical set of scales in New Brunswick.

"I got fed up with being so blankety-blank bloated-looking," she said. "The scales read 150 pounds almost exactly – with the needle very slightly on the fat side."

So she went on a strict diet. "And boy, did I agonize; I was famished!"

After two weeks she stepped on the scales again – "And could you imagine? I still weighed 150, with the needle slightly on the thin side.

"I said the blazes with dieting – life's too short. And for the next two weeks I ate whatever I wanted, strawberries and cream, raspberries and cream, pie, steak, everything.

"At the end of two weeks I got on the scales again – and I'd lost twelve pounds!"

I've told her story to several of my overweight friends.

Not one laughed. They all just stared at me and said: "Can you get me her diet?"

How I Kept
Mr. Jones Alive

I love to call on the sick and brighten them up. In fact, I hurried to see old Mr. Jones, our filing clerk, as soon as he was out of the oxygen tent.

When I told him the office news, he kept dozing off. However, he did show a spark of life during my description of the amusing fight between the office manager and the foundry foreman.

"It started," I said, "over practically nothing – whether Foundry should go on contributing to wreaths for office funerals, when they hardly know us well enough to speak to. Well, *those* two don't speak now, ha, ha!"

Mr. Jones missed the joke altogether. "*Whose* funeral?" the voice from the pillow quavered, gasping.

I patted his head and left quickly, as too much social enjoyment might be tiring him.

A week later Mr. Jones was out of bed and up again, having recovered from a particularly bad spell which came, by coincidence, right after I last saw him. Poor old fellow, he was worrying that the boss might retire him because a mere case of flu hit him so hard.

"No fear," I assured him. "*You're* too valuable. Why, the boss was furious when no one else could locate the Wichita file. He threw files everywhere. We lost a $50,000 order."

Mr. Jones suddenly clutched at his bed and slumped into it. That's how the flu is. You never know when it's coming back.

To give him a laugh – which any doctor will tell you is the best medicine – I related how we stacked up the loose files and letters in a corner and the boss quipped, "They're in better shape now than they've been for years."

Apparently Mr. Jones wasn't listening; he didn't laugh. He just stared glassily at the ceiling and whispered, "Bring . . . me . . . the . . . loose . . . letters."

I brought a few, gladly; there's nothing that speeds up convalescence like feeling useful again.

Next evening I found he had sorted the 900 letters. Wasn't that good? He was flat on his back, looking quite dead, and two doctors were studying him. One said, "It's strange; his strength is ebbing every day." I determined to come in all the oftener to bolster his will to live.

The doctor asked, "Exactly *where* is your distress located now?" He bent down to see if there would be any answer, and then frowned: "He seems to say, 'Under G. . . . Under B. . . . Under K. . . .' Imagines he's playing bingo. Very unusual case."

Unfortunately, I had to take my family on a vacation trip next day. When I returned three weeks later, Mr. Jones was back at work, claiming to feel fine. He really believed it. But when I asked him if he felt complications developing yet, he paled noticeably. I told him, "You're white as a sheet; you're not so well as you think." He gripped his desk to steady himself. "You're overdoing things," I insisted; "that's what finished Uncle Hector, you know." He collapsed over his desk.

This proved what I had just said. Thank goodness I came back in time to straighten him out.

Tell Me Another
TV Sleepytime Story

I t's the strangest thing.

I can fall fast asleep while watching television in the evening just by lying back in a reclining chair and putting my feet up. I can sleep blissfully through every kind of uproar on the tube – earthquakes, tornadoes, volcanic eruptions, the Battle of El Alamein.

In fact, I get so overwhelmed by slumber that even if it's a show I've been waiting up for, I just see the opening titles – and then suddenly the screen credits are rolling by. It's all over.

Yet when at last I give in to my wife's pleas to come to bed – "You can't sleep in that miserable chair all night" – I find I'm unable to sleep in the dark with no bright illuminated screen.

I may lie awake in bed for two hours, because noises bother me.

"Listen to that damn-fool dog," I say, arousing her.

"What dog?"

"Can't you hear it barking?"

After a moment she replies drowsily, "I think so. But it must be a mile away – over at the other side of the river."

"Lord! How do they expect people to get to sleep if they let their dogs keep everyone awake?"

Finally the dog stops barking.

Then I awaken her again and say with a frown, "I hear a cricket out there somewhere."

For some reason she blames my dozing in the chair facing the TV set for the fact that later I can't sleep in bed.

So she now keeps a close watch.

When she catches me sleeping at the end of a program, she shakes my shoulder.

"You were asleep!"

"No I wasn't! I was just thinking with my eyes shut."

"You always snore when you think?"

"Well, in a sort of way – I breathe heavily."

"Then you did follow the program?"

"Of course."

"How did you like it?"

"Fine."

"Did it turn out happily?"

"Yes, very." (This was safe; they all do.)

"Was it a love story?"

"Yes." (They all are.)

Then she swings the haymaker: "You just slept through the bombing of Pearl Harbor."

That's a little sneaky. It's taking unfair advantage of me, because I don't know enough of what went on to defend myself.

I've talked with several friends about how they best drop off to sleep, and I've been surprised to discover: (1) Many follow the same modern technique that I would like to, with a TV set in front of the bed, as opposed to keeping a bedside radio on all night, or reading a book until it crashes to the floor; (2) There are 1,001 traditional other ways to do it.

Some rely on anti-insomnia pills.

Others take a stiff drink, but admit too much only leads to spasmodic, fitful sleep.

"Fifty years ago we always brought our hospital patients a warm glass of milk before bedtime," a retired nurse told me. "But not today – people who can't get to sleep easily are popped a pill."

And counting sheep is out, as far as I'm concerned. I've tried it. Those cussed sheep keep jumping faster and faster over the fence, sometimes three at a time, and one jumps back occasionally, so it's hard mental work to keep count; I become so revved up I can't relax the rest of the night.

One infallible method to drift off to sleep I remember well from my boyhood – but it's a little hard at my age to re-create the circumstances. When I was in high school, I always had lots of pep – until a big exam loomed for the next morning and I realized I'd have to cram my school lessons all evening. This had a magic lulling effect. My feet became leaden at the very thought of it; my head swam. I was exhausted. I could hardly walk to the banister after supper, and drag myself up the stairs, step by step, to my room. There I collapsed into bed and a dreamless sleep after reassuring myself, "I'll get up real early tomorrow morning and study."

What the mind can do and especially how it can operate as a built-in alarm clock are mysteries that medical science is still exploring. For instance, when I was sixteen and working in McAvity's factory office in the summer, I had to catch the six AM train to the city from Ingleside on the St. John River. I set the alarm for five o'clock – and invariably at five seconds before the hour I would awaken just in time to turn the thing off.

Even more baffling was the built-in mental timer of my father-in-law, a Salisbury dairy farmer. When we had to get up at four AM to take a plane out of Moncton, he'd say, "Never mind the alarm clock – I'll wake you up at four. " And he did. He could do it for any hour we chose.

More than a century ago, our great-great-grandparents read advice like this in home medicine books: "Twenty grains carbonate of soda the last thing before going to bed will nearly always cause sleep."

Or this one, whose reasoning puzzles me a little: "As is well known, sleeplessness is usually due to an excess of blood to the brain. To offset this, eat a small raw onion, salted. Again, if stress upon your mind has upset your nervous system, try a light lunch at bedtime, as digesting food brings the blood down into the stomach.

"If you still do not fall asleep, turn down the lights, put an extra pillow under your head, and fix your gaze intently on something to one side of the room. Keep looking at it as your eyes tire, and you will soon drift off to slumber."

Or get a terrible eyestrain headache.

But it's obvious you can help yourself to lapse into sleep by re-creating surroundings that for some reason soothe you.

"I'd like to spend the rest of my life on a train," one man informed me. "The first night I can't sleep at all, but after that I sleep like a top. So I got a gadget to vibrate my bed, and a continuous tape of sound effects like whistles and wheels going clickety-click. It always works."

Then there's a story told to me by a Londoner: "An English sea captain retired to shore after sixty years on the bounding waves, and found he could sleep only if somebody outside kept throwing buckets of water at his windows."

No doubt it would have been too expensive to have people on both sides of the house lifting the sides alternately to simulate a roll.

It's only too bad he lived before the era of the first water beds. If he had one, every time he took a breath he'd pitch and roll and toss, and be completely content – and sleepy.

How the Priddles
Kept Sadie

With the continued rise of inflation, says a news dispatch from Ottawa, it is becoming next to impossible for Canada's householders to hold onto domestic help.

I don't want to see the face of Percy Priddle – who lives just across the street – when he reads that. He's found it hard enough to hold onto Sadie without the inflation spiral getting worse and joining the general conspiracy to take her away.

Sadie arrived sixteen years ago when the kids were ailing and Jean Priddle couldn't handle the work alone.

"This girl Sadie," I remember Percy telling me exultantly, "she's strong, capable, motherly, and smart. And I got her for a fifty-cent want ad! Some bargain, eh?"

As events proved, Sadie was everything Percy said. But I don't remember his ever mentioning the bargain again. In fact, sums like fifty cents just went out of his vocabulary.

They gave Sadie thirty dollars a week and the garret bedroom (this was pretty good for a New Brunswick town in those days; some girls were getting only twenty). Percy was earning sixty-five dollars a week as an architect's assistant, which made him feel capable of affording a maid for a brief emergency at thirty dollars a week, even counting in five dollars more for her food.

New emergencies – mostly new babies – kept coming, however. Very soon Sadie was an indispensable fixture. When she was away every weekend with her folks in the country, a privilege Sadie had insisted on, the house was in turmoil until Sadie returned to take charge and calm the storm.

Christmas, too, was a nightmare, because Sadie wasn't there. "She's never been away from her people at Christmas, or Christmas Eve for that matter," Percy explained to me, almost defensively. He was still very cheery, but I thought I could detect a note of uneasiness in his voice.

From the noisy tumult of the kids across the street on New Year's Day, I judged Sadie had never been away from her people on New Year's either. Before the Priddles knew what was happening to them, Sadie was off every public holiday. Sometimes, when holidays followed weekends, they didn't see her for days at a time. When they heard her opening the front door they wondered who could be walking in and scurried to pick the newspapers off the floor in case it was the minister.

To keep Sadie, you see, they had to keep her happy. The day she learned that Penelope, the girl next door, was making forty dollars a week, they quickly jacked up Sadie's pay and cut down on their movies; as Percy observed, "We'd been going too often anyway."

As soon as Sadie discovered Penelope had every evening off, she got it too, and began earning two dollars a night going out baby-sitting. The Priddles stayed home. I remember Percy saying, "It isn't too bad because, when you come down to it, there's no place like home."

When the glum hint was heard around the kitchen, "Penelope gets two hours' rest every afternoon," the Priddles hurriedly did the same for Sadie to coax her out of her resentful silence, because the seven impressionable children reflected Sadie's moods.

Year by year, Sadie's career followed Penelope's progress. When Penelope took a job in a computer factory, Sadie's salary was raised from forty dollars to sixty to cheer her up and the Priddles sold their car;

"Anyway," as Percy said, "I haven't been getting enough exercise."

It was only to be expected that when Penelope wrote from Ottawa to mention they were paying a hundred dollars a week for maids and Sadie should come up right away, the Priddles hastily offered her a hundred dollars a week to stay. Naturally Jean Priddle had to go back to her old job as a stenographer to do it. There were lots of jobs, because Canada was enjoying industrial expansion, though it can't be said that Percy was enjoying it much. He was now making $130 a week – twice his salary of years ago – but it didn't seem enough to keep a maid on, especially when she ate seven dollars worth of food a week.

Percy finally had to rearrange his job to do his drawing at night so he could be home to help in the daytime; at least, he remarked, there were fewer interruptions at night and you could get more work done. Sadie, you see, didn't get dressed in time for breakfast anymore, because her baby-sitting often kept her out till two AM and, after all, a girl was entitled to eight hours sleep.

She would be silly, Sadie pointed out, to turn down a baby-sitting call worth six dollars with the new double rate after midnight. The Priddles, their resistance completely broken, could only agree she was being very sensible. She did show up every noon to put lunch on the table before her afternoon rest, and she showed up again to prepare supper before leaving for the evening. And, as Percy reminded me, "It's pretty good of her to come back quite frequently on her weekend off just to take the family for a Sunday drive in her new car."

Even with both Priddles working, however, it was difficult to make ends meet, because the seven dollars worth of groceries that Sadie ate now cost twelve dollars.

It was very astute of him the other day, Percy thought, that when Sadie asked if she could have three weeks' holiday with pay – like Penelope – instead of two weeks, he urged her to consider taking four weeks.

172

This would put her one up on Penelope at last – and would also save him the cost of Sadie's food for two extra weeks. And then for a whole month the Priddles could come down out of the refurbished garret, where they now slept, and revel in the luxury of Sadie's downstairs bedroom, which was just as modern as Penelope's except that it didn't have its own bathroom.

Percy felt so good about making two weeks' clear profit on Sadie's food that he yielded to a devilish impulse and went right out and bought himself a package of cigarettes. (He had given up smoking two years ago when Penelope wrote that her Ottawa employer paid her twenty dollars additional weekly for sweeping and dusting her factory office. Percy was smoking too much anyway.)

He even toyed with the idea, Percy told me last week, of telling Sadie to stay with her own folks *all* the time and sending her a paycheque once a week, thus increasing the food savings to $624 a year. But he dropped the idea – "I could see it would be ridiculous to pay anyone for not working at all. Any fool could see that."

Now that the news has come that household help is going to be harder to hold onto than ever, I'm afraid that Percy's enjoyment of his two-weeks food profit is going to be short-lived. If Penelope writes she's turning out a new generation of video games for $395 a week, Percy will have no choice but to put the older kids out to work too. He doesn't want to lose Sadie, because the children love her, and he doesn't dare refuse if she asks for a raise, because the family might find itself out on the street. He hasn't yet got around to telling his wife that Sadie holds the mortgage on the house now.